AN ILLUSTRATED GUIDE TO
HORSES

MARGARET KEENAN

Published in 2009 by TAJ Books International LLP

27, Ferndown Gardens,
Cobham,
Surrey,
UK,
KT11 2BH

www.tajbooks.com

All notations of errors or omissions (author inquiries, permissions) concerning the content of this book
should be addressed to TAJ Books 27, Ferndown Gardens, Cobham, Surrey, UK, KT11 2BH, info@tajbooks.com.

ISBN-13: 978-1-84406-140-2

Printed in China.

AN ILLUSTRATED GUIDE TO
HORSES

MARGARET KEENAN

T&J

INTRODUCTION

The horse is a noble creature and truly one of Nature's greatest achievements. Individual, characterful, magnificent looking, and friendly, a horse can be the best companion anyone can hope for and the bonds of friendship and trust as strong as any. Horses have a long association with humans and their usefulness has proved decisive for people in so many ways, not least for swift travel in the centuries before machinery. Without horses world civilization would have developed totally differently, to point to a few examples: the great Mongol armies would not have swept across the deserts of Asia and through the vast Russian steppes into Western Europe. The Romans would not have been able to establish their empire so securely, and the Wild West of America would have stayed untamed for much longer.

Evolution of the horse

The earliest ancestors of the horse were running around fifty-five million years ago. This was the Eohippus or Hyracotherium, and it was the size of a smallish dog reaching only about 17 inches at the shoulder. It was a shy creature with four toes on its front legs and three toes on its hind legs that helped it to run over boggy, swampy ground and evade capture by bigger, heavier predators. Eohippus survived by eating leaves off huge deciduous and cypress trees of the hot and damp primeval jungles that covered parts of the Earth. Its fossil remains have been found across Europe, in the Wind River Basin in Wyoming, and at the Wasatch Range in Utah.

During the Oligocene Epoch some thirty-seven million years ago, Eohippus migrated across the land bridge linking Europe and North America. Around this period the climate started to change and the swampy jungles began to disappear to be replaced by conifer forests. Eohippus was forced to change its diet to subsist from the new grass pasturelands that were beginning to grow, accordingly the animal changed and evolved over a period of time into Mesohippus. Living about thirty-seven to thirty-two million years ago Mesohippus was a rather larger animal with three toes on all its feet, plus a bigger and stronger set of teeth. With a hotter climate the swamps dried out and Mesohippus started to loose its lateral supporting toes in favor of a stronger and bigger central toe, this began to evolve into the hoof.

In the late Miocene Epoch, seventeen million years ago, across the landmass that became North America, the Merychippus evolved and survived for some five million years on the vast grassy plains that reached to the horizon. With such a diet Merychippus evolved grinding teeth with which to graze the grasslands. By now the horse had doubled in size from its earliest ancestor Eohippus to reach around 35 inches at the shoulder, additionally it had become a more gregarious herd animal that loved to roam the vast grasslands. Furthermore, its lateral toes no longer touched the ground and the primary toe had hardened and thickened into a definable hoof.

The next stage of the horse was the Pliohippus, which lived between six and twelve million years ago. Fossils of Pliohippus have been found in Canada, Nebraska, Dakota, and Colorado. It was in this era that the horse diversified as one branch galloped off into Asia where it evolved as a separate line, while the other remained in North America and drifted down to South American and became in the process the first true monodactyl (one toed) animal in evolutionary history. Pliohippus was by now recognizable as a horse, looking like a smaller version of the animal we know now, with similar teeth and hooves. It was now a swift animal able to outrun its predators, of which there were many. But for unknown reasons its numbers diminished over the course of the next 4,000 years and by around 8,000 years ago it became extinct. Meanwhile, its cousin in Asia, fared a different and altogether happier fate: over time it spread westwards into Europe and south into Africa, all the time evolving into the modern ancestor of the horse.

Domestication of the Horse

Historical research shows that between thirty and forty thousand years ago the horse was unknown in both North and South America, even until relatively recently large parts of the globe were horseless, most notably the entire Americas, sub-Saharan Africa, Australia, and many of the Pacific islands. This meant that in these areas the scattered settlements of hunter-gatherer peoples were diverse and largely unknown to each other, so that when a great civilization such as the Incas, Mayans, or Aztecs arose they were unable to conquer and spread to new areas. Arguably this is also why they fell so easily to the mounted Conquistadors when they arrived in South America.

The earliest history of the horse in relation to people has to rely on interpretations of the archaeological evidence. This appears to show that the horse was domesticated between around 4,000 and 3,000 BC, actually surprisingly slow compared to the fact that dogs had already been assimilated into the human sphere an astonishing nine thousand years earlier and that cattle, sheep and goats had been herded and farmed for some five thousand years. Our Stone Age ancestors regarded the horse as meat and, despite knowing how fast it could run away from the hunt, presumably gave no consideration to its possibilities as a means of transport. Stone Age cave paintings found in Spain and France show horses in hunting scenes, but as objects of prey for the hunt. In Salutre, France a collection of some 10,000 horse skeletons have been discovered at the base of a cliff where Cro-Magnon hunters drove the animals to their death, undoubtedly so that they could eat them.

For around half a million years mankind only saw the horse as a beast of prey. Bronze Age man learnt to herd horses that they still used for meat and perhaps for milk (as the nomads still do), but horses were just farmed animals alongside goats, cattle, and sheep. These early peoples were nomadic, with no written language and very few traces of their lives remain, however, excavations of horse teeth in the Ukraine show evidence of possible bit wear which would date the first known horseback riding to around 4,000 BC. If correct, this means that the nomads in this area had mastered the horse sufficiently to ride it very soon after domestication of the horse, and some three thousand years before proven horseback riding in the Near East.

By 3,000 BC man had discovered the use of the wheel and was more settled in static communities and had started to farm the land by growing grain for rudimentary bread. Then, without having to hunt for food to survive, it is surmised that early man had sufficient time to turn his attention to domesticating the horse.

The first peoples to attempt to tame horses lived in the eastern Ukraine, central Russia, the northern Caucasus, and Kazakhstan and around the steppes to the north of the Black Sea where populations of wild horses roamed free. These peoples in time became famed for their startling rapport with horses, but in the third millennium BC they already harnessed for work oxen, asses and central Asian wild asses called onagers. Here again archaeology implies that these early horses were too small to carry a man and were instead tamed and harnessed to pull wagons and carts.

It stands to reason that if horses were reared and slaughtered for food, little or no rapport would have been built up between herder and animal let alone any longevity in which to build up a relationship of trust and affection, and no affiliated affection would have been passed on by mares to their foals. So perhaps it is not quite so surprising that the horse was domesticated for almost two thousand years before the first indications of horseback riding appear in the archaeological record. Real evidence for the activity only appears towards the end of the first millennium. Then, suddenly, people could travel over far greater distances much quicker than they could walk.

In the Near East particularly around Mesopotamia between 3,000 and 2,000 BC the horse, although not indigenous to the area, first appears as a domesticated draft animal. Initially the horses were harnessed in pairs under an oxen yoke on either side of a pole, with the yoke secured by a strap around the throat. This tended to press on the horse's windpipe and throttled the animals by cutting off their breath. Clearly they required a different arrangement of harness and in time breast straps and collars were developed especially for the draft horse. About 1,500 BC in Egypt a better version of the yoke—the yoke saddle—was devised. This is a Y shaped wooden brace that had the long end lashed to the yoke and the V shape lying across the horse's shoulders so taking the pressure off the animal's windpipe. The yoke saddle rested on pads with the ends joined by crescent-shaped straps that went across the lower part of the horse's throat. The horse existed then as a draft animal for almost a thousand years from the early second millennium BC to the early first millennium BC.

In these early days tractable and rideable horses must have been rare and valuable animals and only the provenance of the powerful and rich. However, as more horses were tamed, mankind's nature being the contentious way it is, made sure that one of the first uses for the horse was as an instrument of war. Chariots and mounted soldiers could move much quicker than the plodding oxen and donkeys of old. Around 1,800 BC the Hittites invented the war chariot and with this near unassailable weapon quickly conquered Mesopotamia and Egypt, in major part thanks to their warhorse training regime. The Hittites put huge highly trained and strictly disciplined chariot forces into battle pulled by well-trained and conditioned horses.

By 1,500 BC the metal bit had been discovered and greatly increased control over the horses. Two different types of bit seem to have been devised at the same time, the jointed bit and the plain bar snaffle and most of them had studs (bit burr's) on the cheek side of the piece in order to alert the horse to directional control: the mouthpieces passed through cheek pieces (except the Scythian bits) where they were secured. Recorded history started in this area and seems to

INTRODUCTION

indicate that driving came well before horseback riding. After 1,000 BC the records talk of well-trained and schooled cavalry that fought in formation. The only riding in this era seems to be by inferior people on donkeys that they controlled through the use of a strap and nose ring.

The bridle first appears on the steppes of southern Russia (as it is now) and was made out of sinew, rawhide, or rope held in place by cheekpieces. Elsewhere, the Scythians are the first great horseback riders of history and made their reputation when they invaded the near East and reaching as far as Palestine. They were skilled archers who fought by firing arrows from the backs of their horses. They were a people for whom horses were a sign of wealth and prestige, they used them as motifs on their jewellery, pottery, and armament, and their belief in the afterlife meant that they were buried with their horses, sometimes a considerable number of them.

With the invention of horse harness men started to use horses in hunting to run down and kill their prey. Suddenly people were able to eat better, hunt further afield, and bring back carcasses from distant parts. Additionally people discovered the fun of horseback riding and soon both the ancient Greeks and Persians were organizing horse races and other equestrian entertainments.

Horses remained the preserve of the wealthy and military right through until the early Middle Ages, leaving donkeys and oxen as the working animals for in agriculture and trade. This was partly because horses required more regular, richer feed, they did not breed as quickly, and were still only relatively small animals and nowhere near as strong as oxen. It took the breeding of heavier horses for this to change. The bloodlines for this came from animals tended by the Germanic tribes who used naturally bigger, stronger horses. The next big step in the progress to the horse as a working animal came with the seemingly obvious development of the shoulder collar (or horse collar) into Europe from China. Now for the first time the horse's entire strength could be put to pulling a plough or hauling wagons.

In ancient China the horse was first domesticated between 3,000 and 2,300 BC during the Lungshan period. The horse was originally introduced into China by central Asian tribes who used horses to draw their chariots. The earliest known Chinese example of a horse-drawn chariot was discovered in the grave of Emperor Wuding, who died in 1118 B.C., but such chariots are thought to have been used for transportation, not as fighting vehicles. Along the Chinese frontiers mounted horses (cavalry) were used to combat the marauding hordes of mounted nomads who, from around the fourth century BC, continually harassed the Middle Kingdom. It is around this period that the stirrup was developed as a way of controling the horse. Initially horses were used almost exclusively by the military and for government service (carrying messages etc) for pulling chariots and neither for general transport nor agriculture. Horses were expensively imported from Central Asia and could therefore only belong to the rich elite and the government.

Across the sea in Imperial Japan the horse seems to have been used by the military from the first century BC thanks to the invading Koreans. Horses enabled mounted warriors to negotiate Japan's rough and mountainous terrain much more easily than before. Imperial communication was also by mounted messenger. Japanese merchants rode horses but had to be led by a footman on either side and so preceded at no greater pace at all because only a soldier was allowed to use his own reins. Meanwhile, Japanese farmers used horses to pull their carts to market. Women, however in both China and Japan rode astride their horse like men (unlike their later sisters in the West).

Arguably the most important invention vis a vie horse harness was that of the stirrup which had arrived in the West by the eighth century, before then riders had far less purchase and solidity which could prove fatal during both the hunt and in battle. The Mongols are credited with devising the stirrup; they were fantastic horsemen who could manoeuver their little horses with amazing skill and athleticism. In fact these skills were crucial to the great Mongol conquests right across Asia and well into western Europe in the 13th century. The use of a stirrup meant that an armed cavalryman could control his mount better and balance himself better so that he could thrust a blow at his opponent and had at least a chance to stay mounted if he took a blow.

The feudal system that developed in Western Europe through the conquests of the Normans made full use of mounted men: it was a requirement that a landowner should supply his lord with so many armored and mounted men depending on his landholdings and rank. The more he supplied, the greater his importance and the higher his rank. For this purpose bigger and stronger horses were bred, until the huge warhorse became a much feared battlefield sight. These giant animals not only had to carry a fully armored knight but also wore armor themselves: these animals were trained to fight and would lash out to deadly effect with their hooves and teeth. Man and horse together had become a truly frightening and effective fighting team.

As Europe settled down to become a more ordered and organized society such heavy cavalry horses were less often needed on the battlefield, instead they became indispensable on the agricultural fields pulling heavy ploughs and carts and dragging heavy wagons across the countryside to market. Even when canals were dug to facilitate the movement of goods heavy horses were employed to pull the boats through the water. Horses had become absolutely indispensable to society and the smooth functioning of civilization at every level.

Xenophon, Father of the "Horse Whisperers"

The Greek historian and philosopher Xenophon, (430–354 B.C.) is cited as the father of classical equitation for his short treatise called The Art of Horsemanship, the oldest instruction manual of its kind, written in about 350 BC. An Athenian and historian, Xenophon was obviously a supreme horseman, and had been in the cavalry before becoming a country gentleman at Scillus, near Olympia on land given to him by Agesilaus, King of Sparta. Unusually, Xenophon encouraged riders to try to understand the mind of their mount and urged readers to be sympathetic to the desires of the horse and build up a relationship of mutual trust and respect. He goes on to give advice on the selection, care and training of horses for use in the military and for utility purposes. He gives details of the principles of classical dressage, and how to train the horse without cruelty. His judgement and advice are still relevant today for the selection and management of a good and happy horse.

The treatise is broken down into twelve chapters starting with "Selecting a Young Horse," with particular attention to the choice of a good mount to ride into battle. The advice includes making sure that the horse is strong and supple with good strong hooves. Part two deals with "Breaking the Colt," the most important point being not to attempt the job yourself but instead acquire a good tempered and gentle young animal. Part three looks at "Selecting an Older Horse," and advises how not to get cheated by buying a horse much older than the owner claims. He says to look at the animal's teeth and, if all the milk teeth have gone, the animal will be older than five and therefore not worth the money. He then goes on to give other pointers as to health, suitability, and obedience. Part four is called "Caring for the Horse," and looks at stabling and caring for the animal's health, in particular taking care of its feet.

Part five, "Grooming the Horse" concentrates on the skill and ability of the groom. How he should care for the animal and his grooming routine. Part six deals with "Grooming and Bridling the Horse Correctly and Safely." How to groom the horse without injury to either horse or groom and in particular not to shout at or frighten the animal. Part seven is called "Mounting, Rider's Position, and Training." Here Xenophon talks specifics on how to mount and ride a horse, how to adjust his reins and how to hold a spear (note that the saddle and stirrups had yet to be invented, so control of the horse was far less assured than in later centuries). Part eight deals with "Advanced Training" with particular reference to warhorses. How to train the animal so that it can ride across rough ground and safely take jumps. He gives a series of exercises for both horse and rider so that they can as safely and comfortably as possible go into battle, and that kindness is the essence of this training.

Part nine describes "Riding the Spirited and Dull Horse." He says be very careful with a spirited horse and above all do not get a spirited horse as a battle mount. Part ten is called "Creating a Showy Horse and Advice on Bitting." He says to avoid the bit and spur, as this will take the enjoyment out of riding for both parties. There is a lot of discussion as to which bit to use and why. Part eleven describes "Creating a Parade Horse," as suitable for state processions and important occasions and how to make the animal rear on command and how to lead the cavalry in an imposing and commanding style. The final and twelfth section is "The Equipment for Battle," and discusses the equipment that both horse and rider need when going into combat. For the rider Xenophon recommends a well-fitting corselet, a good helmet, and gauntlets. While for the horse he suggests using a frontlet, breastplate, and thigh-pieces, as well as something to protect the belly and limbs. As for weapons Xenophon advises taking two javelins made of cornel wood and a sabre. He also describes how to throw the javelins at an enemy.

Horses in the New World

After a gap of some eight thousand years since Pliohippus—one of the earliest ancestors of the horse—became extinct in the Americas. The horse returned with the all-powerful Spanish Conquistadors in the early 1500s. They brought the horses with them across the Atlantic Ocean so that they could explore and conquer new lands; Cortes arrived with sixteen horses, the Native Americans had never seen anything like them and regarded the strangers with awe and in the initial phase of conquest believed that the horse rider and horse were one colossal animal, "horse-men." For these Native Americans the horse was a mysterious and wonderful creature and many of them considered these creatures to be gods. In 1519 Cortes was to exclaim, "Next to God, we owe our victory to our horses."

For the horses themselves the Atlantic crossing could be an extremely traumatic and uncomfortable experience. To combat the effects of pitching and tossing in the rough seas the horses were kept in the near darkness of the hold where they were hung in slings to take the weight off their feet and allow them to sway with the ship's movements. Needless to say on the rougher crossings many horses suffered terribly and sometimes up to half the contingent would die. The dreaded Horse Latitudes of the Atlantic Ocean are so called from the sheer number of dead horses that were thrown over the side into the waters there. Many valuable horses were lost over the passage time.

On arrival in the New World the surviving horses were blindfolded to prevent them panicking and lashing out and then carefully hoisted from the ship's hold and, in the earliest days before wharves, gently lowered into the water from where they had to swim for the shore guided by men in rowing boats. Even this stage could prove problematic for the weakest and most frightened creatures.

Each new boatload of Conquistadors arrived with more horses: in 1519 Coronado set out with 150 horses, and then in 1539 DeSoto's expedition brought 237 horses to the New World. The first governor of the nine provinces of New Spain (later to become Mexico), Antoni de Mendoza had eleven haciendas and over 1,500 horses by 1547. Initially the conquered Indians were not permitted to ride horses unless their masters specifically allowed them to. As for the unconquered peoples, if they were lucky enough to come across a stray horse, they just killed it for food. In time of course the stray horses were collected up and the Native Americans began breeding the animals for their own use.

The garrisoned Spanish horsemen whose job it was to patrol and control the newly conquered lands were issued with the following equipment: a quilted jacket made from elk skins, boots and spurs, saddle bags for carrying water and provisions, a fowling piece and cartridge pouch, plus hanging pistols with holster hooks, a lance, front and rear saddle bows, a buckler, and wooden stirrups.

Colonial America

Horses came with the Settlers and very quickly entire communities and businesses depended on the horse. American horses were soon particularly noted for their quickness and especially their hardiness, unsurprising when one considers that their immediate ancestors had to survive the difficult Atlantic crossing and then quite often unfamiliar and unusually harsh environments. The first truly American breed of horse is the Narragansett Pacer that was originally bred in the Narragansett Bay area of Rhode Island, probably from English and Dutch stock that arrived in Massachusetts in the years between 1629 and 1635. Narragansett Pacers had tremendous endurance, were sure-footed, and moved in a comfortable manner, all of which made them very desirable saddlehorses. They have been described as having a broad back and short legs and moving with a curious rocking movement. For many early colonialists their horse was the only way to get to market or visit friends and transport goods across the rough and ready tracks that passed for roads during the early years.

The English settlers brought their love of fox hunting with them and the first recorded hunt in America was in 1650 when Colonel Robert Brooke brought a pack of hounds to Maryland. The sport proved very popular had many famous followers including George Washington who kept his own hounds and hunters, and Thomas Jefferson who also loved to follow the hounds. Fox hunting was particularly popular in Kentucky and it is no coincidence that this is the area where horse breeding and racing took firmest hold in the United States.

As colonists arrived from Europe and built settlements across New England communication between the burgeoning towns was only possible via water or by using horses. In the early 1600s even Boston and New York were virtually isolated from each other. The start of regular communication between the two cities was through the post when on January 22, 1673 the governor of New York, Francis Lovelace set off the first postal rider the 250 miles to Boston with instructions to visit and offer his services to the various settlements along the way. The rider went from New Haven to Hartford to Springfield, then Bay Path and finally on to Boston: a route dubbed the Upper Boston Post Road. The post rider became the most valuable means of conveying news and information from one settlement to another until the roads improved and stagecoach travel became possible in the late 1700s.

The pioneering breeder of American horses was John Hull, horseman and also treasurer of the Massachusetts Bay Colony. He bought a piece of land on the west side of Narragansett Bay from the local Indians and fenced it off for the specific intent of breeding horses there. During the 1700s Narragansett Pacers were bred in large numbers—as many as a thousand in farms across the Island—to keep up with the demand from other New World colonies, the Caribbean islands, and for essential work on the plantations. Before decent roads connected the towns of colonial America, the saddle horse was the main way of getting around and Rhode Island was the place for providing the horses. But as the roads started to improve people started to give up horseback riding in favor of an easier carriage ride. Trotting became fashionable and the Narragansett Pacer gradually faded from use until it disappeared altogether and became extinct.

As well as the general demand for horses, Rhode Island was the only New England colony to allow official horse racing which was held at a one-mile track at Sandy Neck Beach, South Kingston. Competition to breed the best horses was intense and Rhode Island held on to its reputation for producing the best animals.

In 1667 the English captured New Amsterdam from the Dutch and the following year Governor Nicolls, the first governor of New York, ordered the construction of the first formal racecourse in America. The chosen site was a two-mile course at Salisbury Plain on Long Island and trophies were offered at spring and fall meetings. The governor explained that the purpose of the course was "not so much for the divertissement of youth as for encouraging the bettering of the breed of horses which through great neglect has been impaired." Horseracing quickly became a popular sport and informal races were held everywhere—especially in town streets—at considerable hazard to everyone. In 1674 in Plymouth racing was actually forbidden because of the danger of running horses; a legacy of these times is seen in the name "Race Street" in many New England cities and towns. Even before the Revolution there were 27 stud farms for racehorses around the Potomac, Rappahanock, James, and York rivers.

As soon as horses became ubiquitous the law inevitably started to intervene and various laws were passed concerning the breeding and use or misuse of horses. For instance in 1668 the Massachusetts court ordered that only horses "of comely proportions and 14 hands in stature" were allowed to graze on town commons. Then in 1687 William Penn in Pennsylvania enacted a law saying that only horses

of 13 hands and over were allowed to range free, and that all horses older than 18 months but less than 13 hands high had to be gelded. Furthermore, every horse had to be branded with his owners mark and an owner could only graze on common land twice as many horses as he had in daily use. Such measures indicate that there must have been huge numbers of horses, many of them from indifferent and even poor stock, menacing and over running public grazing lands, and that without branding the strays could not be identified and removed. By 1715 a law was passed in Maryland authorizing the shooting on sight of any stray horses.

By the 1700s it seems that there were so many horses that everyone in America —with the exception of slaves and vagabonds—could have one. At the time it was customary for a traveler to buy a horse for his journey and then on arrival at the destination, sell the animal on.

Horses were instrumental in the growth of the colonies in so many ways, not only carrying pioneers and settlers westwards into the uncharted lands but also as regular means of transporting goods to market. As a consequence of greater prosperity, the roads were improved and a clear communication system grew up around and between the towns and settlements, all of which helped to improve trade even more. Before the use of carriages, a packhorse could only carry around 200 pounds weight of goods over a long distance, which severely hampered the volume of traffic and also the amount of goods a person could take with them as they moved from place to place. Everything changed with the improved roads and mass transit between cities was provided by stagecoaches that offered a swifter and more comfortable means of traveling. Also, westward expansion into the interior of America became much faster.

The Conestoga Wagon was hugely instrumental in this westward expansion of America. It is named after the rich agricultural region settled by German Mennonite immigrants around Conestoga River in Pennsylvania, some 70 miles from Philadelphia. The problem for the farmers here was the difficulty of getting their goods to market in the city and the problems of acquiring supplies. Traditional wagons could not cope with the difficult tracks of the area, so the farmers devised the Conestoga Wagon, a very specific piece of construction as each element of the wagon had to be made from different woods to make the most of their particular properties. The wagon frame was made from oak beams shaped so as to be higher at either end, so that if

INTRODUCTION

the goods shifted during transport they would slide to the center and not endanger the wagon's balance. The sideboards were made from poplar, and the larger than normal wheels hubs were of gumwood with hard hickory spokes. Each piece was carefully chosen, cut, shaped and jointed into position. The whole was covered with a cloth roof of linsey-woolsey (an ancient type of fabric that is woven with a linen warp and a woolen weft) and the wheels were painted bright red with the body of the wagon deep blue. The whole was pulled by a team of six horses.

Throughout this early colonization period the quality of horses varied enormously, but horsemen were working to improve the stock and new breeds soon started to emerge. The Thoroughbred horse was bred in England in the 1700s and soon made its way over to America where its fantastic speed was in great demand for racing. One particular Thoroughbred sire, named Janus, was imported from England to Virginia as a ten-year old in 1756 where he was a successful racehorse before being put to stud for a couple of decades. From his bloodlines the Quarter Horse appeared. Thoroughbred blood improved the emerging American breeds and soon animals like the Quarter Horse and Morgan appeared and then later the Standardbred and American Saddlehorse. Quarter Horses then were crossed with Chickasaw ponies and descendants of the earliest Spanish horses. Quarter Horse racing became very popular and horse racing was the main form of organized sport in America until the mid 19th century.

Native Americans are now synonymous with the horse and it is strange to think that pre-17th century they would never even have seen one, let alone ridden a horse. As previously mentioned, the Spanish Conquistadors even passed laws prohibiting any Indian from riding a horse, instead many Indians especially relished roasted horse flesh. When the Spanish were expelled from New Mexico in 1680 by the Pueblo Indians they left behind many of their horses, some were eaten, a few ridden, but most were used for trade with the Plains Indians in return for cloth and jerked buffalo meat. Plains Indians instead of eating the horses learned to ride them and fight from their backs in swiftly moving groups. Almost immediately the Plains way of life changed as they benefited from the vastly greater mobility they gained from their horses. Those tribes that had horses were able to dominate the tribes who remained on foot, and the Plains Indians soon garnered a reputation for being great buffalo hunters and became rich on the trade they could get for their meat and hides.

Horse Breeds

There are many different breeds of horse. Generally, a horse is defined by its size, namely that a horse has to be over 14.2 hands at maturity. However this definition is not watertight as a number of other characteristics have to be taken into account and in fact there are a number of breeds that are naturally much smaller (pony sized) but are still classified as horses.

There are many registered breeds and in common with registers of dogs and cats some authorities recognize certain breeds that other do not.

The Przewalski Horse

Despite only being discovered in 1879 the Przewalski Horse (Equus Przewalski) is believed to be the living link with the distant horse depicted in cave paintings made by Cro-Magnon man 18,000 years ago in Lascaux, France. Moreover, the Przewalski horse is thought to be either a direct or collateral ancestor of many living equine breeds. Discovered still living in remotest Mongolia on a diet of tamarisk, feather grass, and rhubarb roots, the Przewalski was in imminent danger of extinction. Once living in large herds led by a dominant male, the Przewalski declined due to a combination of extremely harsh winters, hunting, and competition with domesticated livestock for water and pasture. Survival programs were put place to attempt to reverse its dire situation. Should the worst happen, a few animals are also protected in zoos around the world.

Named for its discoverer, a Russian captain called Nikolai Mikailovich Przewalski, this small horse is remarkably similar to the prehistoric cave paintings. Known as the Taki, Tachi, or Tag to Mongolians, the Przewalski has never been reliably tamed and has to be approached with caution as it can be vicious. This horse typically stands between 12 and 14 hands high, has a light colored muzzle, and a dun hide with dark legs and a dark streak that runs from its hind quarters all the way up to its short, upstanding mane. It lacks a forelock.

Color Breeds

Horses that are registered in this category include the Pinto Horse, the Palomino, and the Buckskin. Qualification for this registry differs, some authorities will accept any breed of horse provided that it has the correct stipulated coloring and others' won't. Furthermore the foals from a registered pairing will not automatically qualify as a color breed, the foal has to have the correct coloring or markings to be accepted onto the register.

However, some color breeds always breed true and do not loose their breed characteristics, these are the Appaloosa, the American Paint Horse, and the Friesian Horse. The former is an interesting case, because it is a spotted horse native to the American West and is descended from carefully chosen animals selectively bred by the Nez Perce Indians of Idaho, Oregon, and Washington. Over the centuries the Appaloosa bloodlines became diluted until in 1938 the Appaloosa Horse Club was established to restore and reinvigorate the breed. Distinctive characteristics were established, including strong legs and quarters and vitally, spotted coloring. Varied patterns and colors were established, such as the blanket, leopard, snowflake, and marbleized roan. Animals that stand less than 14 hands at maturity cannot be registered.

Different breeds of horses have their advocates and admirers and some of them possess virtues that others don't. Some breeds cope better with rough terrain, others have the ability to keep going in even the hottest weather, while others have a thick pelt designed to keep out the winter ice and snow. When deciding on what type of horse to get a great deal depends on the kind of conditions it will be ridden in and the local environment and weather conditions.

The complete list of horse breeds recognized in the United States in alphabetical order is as follows: Abaco Barb, Abtenauer, Aegidienberger, Akhal-Teke, Albanian, Altai, Alter Real, American Cream Draft, American Paint Horse, American Quarter Horse, American Saddlebred, Andalusian horse, Andravida, Anglo-Arabian, Appaloosa, Arappaloosa, Arabian horse, Ardennes (or Arednnais), Argentine Criollo, Ariegeois, Asturcon, Australian Stock Horse, Auxois, Aveligrese, Azerbaijan, Azores, Azteca.

Baise, Baleraric, Bali, Balikun, Baluchi, Ban-ei, Banker Horse, Barb, Bashkir, Bashkir Curly, Basuto, Batak, Bavarian Warmblood, Belgian, Belgian Warmblood, Bhutia, Bosnian, Boulonnais, Brabant, Brandenburger, Brazilian Sport Horse (aka Brasileiro de Hipismo), Breton (or Trait Breton), Brumby, Budyonny (or Budenny), Buohai, Buryat, Byelorussian Harness.

Calabrese, Camargue, Campolina, Canadian Horse, Cape Horse, Carthusian, Caspian, Chilean, Chilote, Cleveland Bay, Clydesdale, Colonial Spanish, Colorado Ranger, Criollo, Danish Warmblood, Deliboz, Dole Trotter (or Dole Gudbrandsdal), Don, Dutch Warmblood, Drovian, Falabella, Finnish, Fleuve, Fjord horse (aka Norwegian Fjord Horse), Florida Cracker Horse, Fouta (or Foutanké), Frederiksborg, Freiberger, Friesian horse, Furioso.

Groningen, Gypsy Vanner, Hackney, Haflinger, Hanoverian, Heck, Holsteiner, Hungarian Warmblood. Iberian horses (Andalusian, Alter Real, Lusitano and crosses), Icelandic, Irish Draught, Irish, Irish Hunter, Jutland , Kabardian (or Kabardin), Karabakh, Kathiawari, Kentucky Mountain Saddle Horse, Kiger Mustang, Kisber Felver, Kladruber, Kinsky-horse, Knabstrup, Konik, Kustanair.

Latvian Harness Horse, Lipizzan (or Lipizzaner), Lithuanian Heavy Draught, Lokai, Lusitano, Malapolski, Mangalarga Marchador, Mangalarga, Maremmana, Marwari, M'Bayar, Messara, Mezöhegyesi sport-horse (sportló), Mongolian, Metis Trotter, Miniature horse, Missouri Fox Trotter, Morab, Morgan, Moyle, Mustang, Murgese, Narragansett Pacer, National Show Horse, Nez Perce Horse, Nonius, Nordlandshest, Noriker, Norwegian Fjord, Novokirghiz.

Oldenburg (or Oldenburgh), Orlov trotter, Paso Fino, Percheron, Peruvian Paso (aka Peruvian Stepping Horse, Pleven, Pinzgauer, Przewalski (or Takhi), Qatgani, Quarab, Quarter Horse, Racking horse, Rocky Mountain, Russian Don, Russian Trotter, Salerno, San Fratello, Sardinian (or Sardinian Anglo-Arab), Selle Francais, Shire horse, Shagya Arabian, Sorraia, Spanish Mustang, Spanish Tarpan, Spotted Saddle horse, Sokolsky, Soviet Heavy Draft, Standardbred, Suffolk Punch, Swedish Ardennes, Swedish Warmblood, Swiss Warmblood.

Tennessee Walker, Tersk, Thoroughbred, Tiger Horse, Trait Du Nord, Trakehner, Turkoman (or Turkemene), Ukrainian Riding Horse, Vlaamperd, Waler (aka Australian Waler), Walkaloosa, Welsh Cob, Westphalian, Wielkopolski, Windsor Grey, Württemberger (or Württemberg), Yili, and finally the Yonaguni.

Mythological Horses

Horses have always held a special place of reverence in men's hearts even from the earliest cave man era, so it is no surprise that these magnificent creatures hold a special place in world mythology. Our ancient ancestors ascribed different qualities to the animals they saw around them and the horse invariably represents swiftness, but also intelligence, power, and almost above all, beauty. Horses play important roles in many ancient myths but some animals play center stage and perhaps the most prominent mythological horse in the western canon is Pegasus.

Greek legend says that Poseidon, the Greek god of the sea, was as was the way with Greek gods, frequently unfaithful to his wife Demeter. One of many variants of the story says that after a complicated escapade when Poseidon disguised himself as a stallion (a frequent disguise) to seduce the Gorgon Medusa, she became pregnant with the winged horse Pegasus and his brother the giant, Chrysaor. In time the goddess Athena managed to catch and tame Pegasus and then gave him as a gift to the Muses at Parnassus; as their magnificent winged horse he became the messenger and servant of the poets. In addition, legend says that wherever his hoof struck the ground a freshwater spring appeared.

Pegasus carried the hero Bellerophon during his fight against the fearsome Chimera. First Bellerophon had to capture Pegasus and the most popular myth says that the goddess Athena left him a golden bridle while he slept with instructions to slip it over the horse's neck while he drank at the well at the citadel of Corinth. Once securely mounted Bellerophon sought out the Chimera and with the invaluable help of his winged horse, defeated him. In Classical times Bellerophon transmuted into the hero Perseus who slew the Gorgon Medusa with the help of Pegasus.

Another mythological horse was the Centaur that had the torso, arms, and head of a man with the body of a horse. Centaurs were usually portrayed as rowdy, untrustworthy creatures who drank far too much but nevertheless possessed enormous physical strength and intelligence. They were often troublesome creatures but the Centaur Chiron was a gentle teacher and healer who ultimately sacrificed his immortal life to provide mankind with the gift of fire. By way of thanks the ancient Greeks said he found immortality in the stars as the constellation Sagittarius, in more recent times he has become associated with the southern hemisphere constellation Centaurus.

Chapter six of the Bible in the Book of Revelation talks of the Four Horsemen of the Apocalypse who brought devastation to mankind. Each of the horsemen represents an ultimate evil, War, Famine, Pestilence, and Death. The first horseman, Pestilence, rides a white horse, represents "Conquest," and carries a bow. The second horseman, War, rides a red horse and carries a killing sword. The third horseman, Famine, rides a black horse and carries a set of scales. The fourth horseman, Death, rides a pale sickly yellow horse and trails death in his wake.

For the ancient Gauls the fertility goddess Epona, the "Divine Mare," was also the deity of horses, donkeys, and mules. When the Romans conquered Gaul they assimilated Epona into their pantheon and she became Romanized and adopted as the goddess and protector of the Roman cavalry and in particular the Imperial Horse Guard. With their promotion the cult of Epona spread right across the Roman empire.

"Leucippotomy" is the ancient English practice of cutting the image of a horse into the white chalk hillside. These hill figures—many of them are in the shape of men—are intended to be seen from a distance and a lot of them are truly ancient. Self-evidently only seen in limestone landscapes the county of Wiltshire is particularly rich in these images. There are white horses cut into the hills at Alton Barnes, Wiltshire (1812), Broad Town, Wiltshire (1864), Cleadon Hills, Tyne and Wear (pre-1887), Old Devizes aka the Snobs' horse (1845), New Devizes (1999), Cherhill/Oldbury, Wiltshire (1780), Folkestone, Kent (2003) Hackpen/Broad Hinton/Winterbourne Bassett, Wiltshire (c.1838), Hindhead, Surrey (pre-1913 but now lost), Ham Hill/Inkpen, Wiltshire (1865-1877), Kilburn, Yorkshire (1857), Old Litlington, Sussex (c.1838), New Litlington, Sussex (1925), Marlborough/Preshute, Wiltshire (1804), Osmington, Dorset (c.1808), old Pewsey, Wiltshire (1785), new Pewsey, Wiltshire (1937), Rockley, Wiltshire (discovered 1948, now lost), Tan Hill, Wiltshire (now lost), Uffington (Bronze Age, 1400 BC to 600 BC), Oxfordshire, Westbury, Wiltshire (pre-1742). These chalk figures last for as long as people are willing to go out and renew them by cutting the turf and refreshing the chalk. Thus they become "lost" when local people for a variety of reasons fail to look after their hill figures.

The Uffington White Horse in Oxfordshire is cut into the side of Uffington Castle, an Iron Age hill fort and is some 374 feet (110 m) long. It is best viewed from a distance and might have been cut as a tribal symbol or to represent a Celtic god. However, local people have for centuries held the opinion that it is in fact the dragon that St George slew on nearby Dragon Hill. In 1994 an archaeological investigation used a dating process based on optically stimulated luminescence that dated the figure to some three thousand years ago.

Getting started

The ultimate pleasure of a horse is riding it, but like any deceptively easy-looking pastime it is a skill that needs to be learnt and practised. This not only requires an understanding of your mount and its needs but also of your body and your needs, without both of which it can be very easy to injure yourself or your horse.

There are many benefits from a close association with horses. Research has proved that even stroking and patting a horse can reduce stress and lower blood pressure. The physical demands of horseback riding are very beneficial as the constant changing movements help to build up deep postural muscles, furthermore, horseback riding is one of the very few sports that works the muscles of the inner thigh. In fact overall, riding has been proved very beneficial in producing overall aerobic fitness and that a fairly demanding ride is the equivalent to brisk running.

Any novice rider is well advised to find a good teacher, especially one who specializes in training beginners and who will provide well tempered, amenable horses who won't misbehave and take advantage of a novice rider. Riding schools are found all over the place and like any such institutions vary considerably in quality, although one thing they almost certainly will be is costly. Ask around and check local horse associations for recommended teachers. If you have the time a good way to learn to ride is by taking a riding holiday, this is also a great way to "get back in the saddle" and to improve rusty riding skills. One of the advantages of a riding school is that they will be able to provide suitable gear—it's better not to invest in expensive riding outfits before you discover whether or not you will enjoy horseback riding. The most important equipment is a hard hat that should fit comfortably and securely, if it is too loose it won't properly protect your head if you fall off. Some schools also recommend the use of a body protector that protects the back and chest area in the event of a fall. Comfortable, well-fitting trousers neither too tight nor too loose are needed so that they neither hinder nor hamper movement. Additionally, good leather gloves with a good grip are important for holding onto the reins, especially if they become wet and slippery or if the horse has a tendency to pull. The correct footwear is also important, proper horsemen wear jodhpur boots or long boots but a beginner can get away with sensible shoes that have a small heel for bracing against the stirrup iron. Riding a horse requires a good sense of balance and physical awareness so

that with practice both horse and rider move together smoothly and comfortably. A good instructor will supply confidence to both animal and rider making the whole experience enjoyable and rewarding. The first thing to be taught is good posture on the animal, not too stiff and not too floppy; bad posture will give the rider back problems and could also damage the horse. Teachers know that the commonest mistake among beginners is stiffness that causes awkward jolting as the horse moves. This is often caused by nerves but also in older riders can be due to a general lack of suppleness. Simple bending exercises can alleviate this, particularly ones that work on the lower back, hips, shoulders, and ankles. In fact disciplines such as Pilates and yoga are ideal for alleviating such problems.

It is said that riders with a natural sense of rhythm will pick up riding much more easily than other people. This is because when a horse trots it is described as moving in a "two-time" rhythm, so the rider must learn to rise up out of the saddle on the first beat and sink back into the saddle on the second. This can take a bit of concentration at first but soon becomes second nature and requires no thought at all as man and horse move smoothly together. It is important to have mastered these basics and be able to confidently handle the horse; your mount will be happier and more assured if he feels that you are secure in your abilities. The horse can sense whether or not you are relaxed and your nerves will translate to him if you are afraid. The next stages are walking, trotting, and cantering when they are smoothly accomplished it is time to attempt the first jump. A good instructor will tell you to lean slightly forward but remain balanced with your thighs at a more horizontal angle. Try to flow with the movement of the horse and only attempt a small jump to begin with.

Of course the most expensive aspect of learning to ride successfully can be the overwhelming desire to own your own horse, a very expensive business altogether!

Famous Horses

Many great warrior leaders are closely associated with their horse and in fact the animal is more often than not credited with saving the man's life by way of some astonishing feat of bravery or athleticism. It is only in the last hundred years or so that the horse has been superseded by machines during the great battles of history; until the invention of the locomotive, internal combustion engine, and airplane the easiest and

INTRODUCTION

quickest way of moving soldiers from one location to another has been through the use of horses. Inevitably horses have historically been some of the most numerous casualties of war and their almost total disappearance from the conflict zones of the world is one of the most marked differences of modern warfare. Great military leaders required big, brave, resilient mounts and a number of horses have become synonymous with their riders.

The greatest horse of antiquity is the magnificent stallion Bucephalus, the favourite horse of Alexander the Great. While he was still only a twelve year old and as yet untried in battle, Alexander spotted a particularly beautiful young horse running with his father's herd. The horse had been offered to his father Philip II by a Thessalian horse dealer called Philoneicus, but much to Philip's annoyance the horse had proved unbreakable so it was left to roam with the wild horses. Alexander was determined to have the black horse with a white star and from close observation noticed that the animal shied away from its own shadow, so when he approached it he positioned himself so that the horse's shadow fell behind him. Slowly Alexander gained the animal's trust and was able, much to his father's annoyance, to ride the beautiful creature. Alexander named the horse Bucephalus, because his head was broad like a bull's. Bucephalus would allow no one else to ride him and he carried Alexander for thousands of miles into battle all the way from Greece to Egypt and on to India. Bucephalus eventually died aged somewhere between 28 and 30 of wounds sustained during the Battle of the Hydaspes in June 326 BC (now in modern Pakistan), ironically this was also to be Alexander's last battle. Bucephalus was reputedly buried in Jalalpur Sharif outside of Jhelum in Pakistan. In honor of his remarkable horse Alexander named a city Bucephala after him; although now lost, it is thought to be the modern town of Jhelum.

Another famous battle horse was Copenhagen, the mount of the Duke of Wellington and named for his victory at the Battle of Copenhagen. The horse was a 15 hands high chestnut and carried the Iron Duke in the Battle of Waterloo, "from four in the morning till twelve at night." Eventually pensioned off to grass at Strathfieldsaye it died in 1835, at the age of twenty-seven, and was buried with military honours. Statues of the Duke invariably show him mounted on Copenhagen.

The name of one of the great horses of American history is unknown, and it may be that she never had a name (as was the practice of the time). However, the name Brown Beauty is most commonly ascribed to the plucky mare that the great patriot Paul Revere rode for his midnight ride during the American Revolution. On the night of April 18-19 Paul Revere and William Dawes were ordered to take the news from Boston to Lexington to warn the Minutemen of the arrival of the British army to arrest John Hancock and Samuel Adams and their intention of moving on to seize weapons stored in Concord.

Revere first had to cross the Charles River to Charleston while Dawes was sent on the longer land route. In Charleston Revere borrowed a brown mare from John Larkin, a sympathetic Charleston merchant. Brown Beauty—reputed to be a Narragansett Pacer—was saddled up and at about eleven o'clock the pair set off. Outrunning two patrols and narrowly avoiding capture, Revere rode through towns that have now become Somerville, Arlington, and Medford, warning patriots along the way of the advancing British. He arrived at Lexington at about midnight, warned Adams and Hancock, and after a short rest accompanied Dawes (who had arrived half an hour later) to Concord, but they were stopped by a British patrol along the way at Lincoln. Revere had Brown Bess confiscated and he eventually walked back to Lexington arriving just in time to witness the start of the battle. Brown Bess was never returned to her owner and her ultimate fate is unknown but she is immortalized in Henry Longfellow's poem "Paul Revere's Ride."

George Washington was a great horseman whose favorite mount was a chestnut hunter called Nelson who he had received as a gift from Thomas Nelson Jr., the governor of Virginia. Before the Revolution Washington rode Nelson to hounds for ten years and then took him on campaign during the war and despite near starvation at Valley Forge and endless marches from Boston to the Carolinas survived the ordeal to see his master become the first president of the United States.

During the Civil War the bravest and best rider of all was Union general Ulysses S Grant. He was reputedly a very fine horseman especially known for his endurance and speed, and particularly liked big, powerful and spirited horses. Even while a cadet at West Point Academy he had been noted as a particularly brave and fine horseman. Throughout his career he rode a number of big horses but his undisputed favorite was Cincinnati, a remarkable horse that he came by through a strange set of circumstances after the Battle of Chattanooga when he was in St Louis visiting his sick son Frederick. While there he was the recipient of a letter from a Mr S.S. Grant, co-incidentally his dead brother's initials, who asked him to come and see him while laid up ill in the Lindell Hotel. Grant was intrigued and went along and met the man who said that he possessed the finest horse in the world but that as he could never ride again he would like to give the horse to General Grant, knowing how much he liked a spirited horse. But Grant had to promise that he would give the horse a good home, never mistreat him, and never allow anyone to mistreat him. Grant agreed, accepted the horse with thanks, and named him Cincinnati.

The great Southern General Robert E Lee's most famous horse was called Traveller. He was discovered and bought for $175 in the fall of 1861 for use as a battle mount by Major Thomas L. Broun. Originally called "Jeff Davis" the horse was born in 1858 and raised on the green grass of Blue Sulphur Springs, in Greenbrier county, Virginia (now West Virginia). The gray steed caught the eye of General Robert E Lee with its bold carriage and obvious strength and power and he eventually bought it from Major Broun in 1862 for $200 and it served him well through the war. He called the horse Traveller—he intentionally spelt the name in the English fashion with a double "l." Soon after the Battle of Malvern Hill Lee started to use Traveller regularly because although he was spirited and nervous he had no defects. During the second Battle of Manassas while General Lee was reconnoitring at the front, after dismounting Lee was holding onto the reins when something startled Traveller and he plunged violently throwing Lee to the ground where he broke both his hands. During his recuperation he used smaller, quieter horses but returned to riding Traveller until the end of the war. Most famous horses are inextricably linked with the names of their riders and together they have made their name in history. Trigger (1932-1965) was the palomino companion and friend of movie star cowboy Roy Rogers, he stood at 15.3 hands and was out of a Thoroughbred stallion and a Quarter Horse mare and was a beautiful golden Palamino with a white mane and tail. In the 1950s the pair moved into television with a successful series. Trigger was "spotted" in 1938 when he was still called Golden Cloud and the mount of Olivia de Havilland in The Adventures of Robin Hood . He was first used by Roy Rogers as support for his first starring role in Under the Western Stars (1939). When Rogers fell out with the studio they threatened to take Trigger away from him but he claimed that he had already bought him for $2,500. Subsequently Trigger appeared alongside Rogers in all his movies and tv series and went on to become the best known and most popular horse in the entertainment industry. Another similarly popular and famous horse was Silver, the white stallion mount of the Lone Ranger. Often at the start of both the radio and tv show the announcer orated, "A fiery horse with the speed of light, a cloud of dust, and a hearty Hi-yo Silver!" The Lone Ranger was accompanied by his Native American friend and helper, Tonto, and his Pinto horse called Scout. In 1957 Silver won the Patsy Award for Excellence given to outstanding tv and movie animal actors.

Popular movie and tv cowboy Gene Autry was almost always accompanied by a horse called Champion, although in truth they were three different horses, the best of which was a Tennessee Walking Horse. Champion even had his own tv series, The Adventures of Champion which first aired on CBS network from September 1955 through February 1956. Champion also starred in his own comic series.

Another horse with his own tv show was Mister Ed but he wasn't a cowboy horse, he was a talking (and singing) horse, but only to his owner Wilbur Post. The series aired in the early to mid 1960s and was hugely popular. The horse playing Mr Ed was a beautiful palomino American Saddlebred called Bamboo Harvester whose lips moved as he spoke . He died quietly without publicity in 1970 at the age of 19.

For many centuries horses were vital to almost every economy and business in the civilized world. City streets thronged with horses and entire communities depended on horses for their living, not just for transport and carriage but for the saddle-makers, ostlers, stable boys, farriers, horse feed suppliers, carriage makers, and horse doctors. With the invention of the combustion engine the horse has all but disappeared from our city streets, entire skills and industries have virtually gone. Horses are now mostly kept for pleasure rather than necessity, for the joy of riding them and for the pleasure of their company. Very few horse relatively now have to earn their living and most of those that do are involved in the horse racing industry and lead largely pampered and indolent lives. These beautiful, intelligent creatures are still important elements in everyday life for many people and long may they remain so.

AKHAL-TEKE

The Akhal-Teke, 'Ahalteke' in the Turkmen language, horse breed is a breed of horse from Turkmenistan, where they are a national emblem. They are noted for their speed and for endurance on long marches. These "golden-horses" are adapted to severe climatic conditions and are thought to be one of the oldest surviving horse breeds. There are currently about 3,500 Akhal-Tekes in the world, mostly in Turkmenistan and Russia, although they are also found in Germany and the United States. Many Akhal-Tekes are bred at the Tersk stud in the northern Caucasus Mountains. The Akhal-Teke usually stands between 14.3 and 15.2 hands. The horses are usually a pale golden color somewhat akin to buckskin, with black points. They can also be bay, black, chestnut, or grey. The Akhal-Teke's most notable and defining characteristic is the natural metallic bloom of its coat. This is especially seen in the palominos and buckskins, as well as the lighter bays, although some horses "shimmer" more than others.

The Akhal-Teke has a fine head with a straight or slightly convex profile, and long ears. It also has almond-shaped eyes. The mane and tail is usually sparse. Their long back is lightly muscled, and is coupled to a flat croup and long, upright neck. The Akhal-Teke possesses a sloping shoulder and thin skin. These horses have strong, tough, but fine limbs. They have a rather slim body and ribcage (like an equine version of the greyhound), with a deep chest. The conformation is typical of horses bred for endurance over distance. The Akhal-Tekes are lively and alert, with a reputation for being "one-rider" horses. The breed is tough and resilient, having adapted to the harshness of Turkmenistan lands, where horses must live without much food or water.

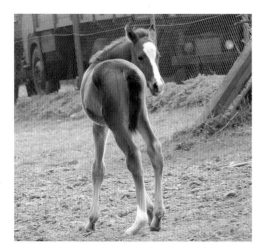

AMERICAN QUARTERHOUSE

The American Quarter Horse is a breed of horse originally bred for sprinting short distances, typically races of a quarter mile or less. The Quarter Horse is the most popular breed in the United States, and the American Quarter Horse Association is the largest breed registry in the world, with over 3.2 million Quarter Horses registered worldwide. It is commonly believed to be the world's fastest horse over short distances, and has been clocked at 55 mph. The Quarter Horse is well known both as a race horse and for its performance in rodeos, horse shows and as a working ranch horse. The compact body of the Quarter Horse is well-suited to the intricate and speedy maneuvers required in calf roping, reining, cutting, working cow horse, barrel racing and other western riding events, especially those involving live cattle. The versatile Quarter Horse is also shown in English disciplines, driving, and many other equestrian activities.

The modern American Quarter Horse has a small, short, refined head with a straight profile, and a strong, well-muscled body, featuring a broad chest and powerful, rounded hindquarters. They usually stand between 14 and 16 hands high, although some Halter-type horses may grow as tall as 17 hands. There are two main body types: the stock type and the hunter or racing type. The stock horse type is shorter, more compact, stocky and well muscled, yet agile. The racing and hunter type Quarter Horses are somewhat taller and smoother muscled than the stock type, more closely resembling the Thoroughbred. Quarter Horses come in nearly all colors. The most common color is sorrel, a brownish red, part of the color group called chestnut by most other breed registries.

ANDALUSIAN

The Andalusian horse or Spanish horse is one of the oldest breeds of horses in the world today. Andalusians have been used for all manner of riding horses, and were the preferred mount of kings over many centuries. They excel in high school dressage and are used in cattle work and bullfighting in their native Spain. Partbred Andalusians are popular as sport horses in many countries. They also excel at classical dressage and are used for show jumping and other equestrian activities.

Andalusians are strongly-built, compact horses, generally standing 15.2-16.2 hands. They move with a high, elegant action, which makes them particularly suitable for Haute École (or High School) Dressage. They usually have a lean, medium-length head with a convex profile and large eyes, a long but broad and sometimes cresty neck (particularly in stallions), a long, sloping shoulder, clean legs with good bone, short, strong cannons, and a thick, long, flowing mane and tail. The Andalusian has a reputation for a proud but cooperative temperament, sensitive and intelligent, able to learn quickly and easily when treated with respect and care. Andalusian horses today are found in a number of colours although the most common colour, seen in about 80% of all Andalusians, is grey. There are also purebreds who are bay, black, and chestnut. Other colours, such as palomino, are not recognized as a legal colour for Andalusians in most countries, as the presence of the dilution gene that creates the colour is considered evidence of crossbreeding. However these colours are recognized in the Lusitano breed of Portugal, descended from the Andalusian horse.

ANGLO ARABIAN

The Anglo-Arabian horse is what its name implies: a Thoroughbred (prefix Anglo) crossed with an Arabian horse. The cross can be made between a Thoroughbred stallion and Arabian mare, or vice-versa. It can also be a cross between a Thoroughbred and an Anglo-Arab, an Arabian and an Anglo-Arab, or between two Anglo-Arabians. This produces a cross that is generally more substantial than a pure-bred Arabian. No matter what the cross, the Anglo-Arabian must have at least 25 percent Arabian blood to be considered an Anglo-Arabian.

The Anglo-Arabian has been used for the military, as well as a general riding and sport horse. It also has influenced France's main sport horse breed: the Selle Francais. The breed is also excellent at eventing, with the stamina, jumping ability, and speed needed for this demanding sport. As a result of the different crosses that can be made to produce an Anglo-Arabian, their size and appearance is variable. The largest horses are usually produced by breeding a Thoroughbred mare to an Arabian stallion. The best examples of this breed inherit the endurance and stamina of the Arabian, and the speed and scope of the Thoroughbred. The horses are usually 15.2-16.3 hands high, and mainly chestnut, bay or brown. The best of the breed have more of an Arabian-type conformation, with a long neck, prominent whithers, a short and strong body, more sturdy than the Thoroughbred, and a deep chest. It should not look like a Thoroughbred, nor an Arabian. They have fine heads, although not overly dished in profile, and have strong bone.

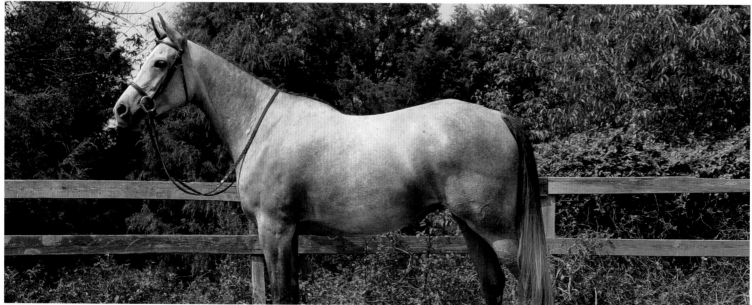

APPALOOSA

The Appaloosa is a horse breed with a color preference. It is best known for a distinctive leopard spotted coat color pattern, but also has other distinctive physical characteristics. The Nez Perce tribe of the American Pacific Northwest developed the breed. They were once referred to by white settlers as the "Palouse horse," probably because the Palouse River ran through the heart of Nez Perce country. Gradually, the name evolved into "Appaloosa." Most Appaloosas are recognized by their colorful spotted coat patterns, striped hooves, mottled skin (most visible around their eyes and on their muzzle) and white sclera around the eye. Appaloosas can have brown, blue or hazel eyes. Sometimes they will have eyes of different colors. However, some Appaloosas do not display all of the typical traits and may appear to be "solid" (without spots, visible coat pattern or other characteristics generally associated with the breed.) While the original, "old time" Appaloosas often had a sparse mane and tail, it was not a predisposition for the breed as a whole; many original Appaloosas had full manes and tails. Today the "rat tail" trait is usually bred away from and most "modern" Appaloosas have full manes and tails.

The overwhelming majority of Appaloosas now seen in the horse show ring today have an athletic build that resembles that of the Appendix Quarter Horse and hunter type Thoroughbred. Excessive heavy muscling is not desired, as slow twitch muscles hinder a horse's speed and manoeuvrability. The middle of the road "stock horse" build is well suited to western riding disciplines such as cutting, reining, rodeo and O-Mok-See sports such as barrel racing (Camas Prairie Stump Race) and pole bending (Nez Percé Stake Race) as well as short-length horse racing, generally at the quarter-mile distance.

ARABIAN

The Arabian horse is a breed of horse with a reputation for intelligence, high spirit, and outstanding stamina. With a distinctively chiseled head and high tail carriage, the Arabian is one of the most easily recognizable horse breeds in the world. Arabians are one of the oldest horse breeds. There is archaeological evidence of horses that resemble modern Arabians dating back 4,500 years. Throughout history, Arabian horses from the Middle East spread around the world by both war and trade, used to improve other breeds by adding speed, refinement, endurance, and good bone. Today, Arabian bloodlines are found in almost every modern breed of riding horse.

Arabian horses have refined, wedge-shaped heads, a broad forehead, large eyes, large nostrils, and small muzzles. Most display a distinctive concave or "dished" profile. Many Arabians also have a slight forehead bulge between their eyes, called the "jibbah" by the Bedouin, that adds additional sinus capacity, believed to have helped the Arabian horse in its native dry desert climate. Another breed characteristic is an arched neck with a large, well-set windpipe set on a fine, clean throatlatch. This structure of the poll and throatlatch was called the mitbah or mitbeh by the Bedouin, and in the best Arabians is long and somewhat straight, allowing flexibility in the bridle and room for the windpipe. Other distinctive features are a relatively long, level croup and naturally high tail carriage. Well-bred Arabians have a deep, well-angled hip and well laid-back shoulder. Most have a compact body with a short back. Some, though not all, have 5 lumbar vertebrae instead of the usual 6, and 17 rather than 18 pairs of ribs. Thus, even a small Arabian can carry a heavy rider with ease.

AUSTRALIAN BRUMBY

A Brumby is a free-roaming feral horse in Australia. Although they are found in many areas around the country, the most well-known brumbies are found in the Australian Alps region in south-eastern Australia. Today, the majority of them live in the Northern Territory, with the second largest population in Queensland. There are more horses in the wild in Australia than any other country, outnumbering even the American Mustang. A herd of brumbies is known as a "mob" or a "band."

Brumbies are the descendants of escaped or lost horses, dating back, in some cases, to those belonging to the nation's early European settlers. These horses included the "Capers" that arrived from South Africa, Timor Ponies from Indonesia, British pony breeds, various British draft horse breeds and a significant number of Thoroughbreds and Arabians. Today they live in many places, including some National Parks. Occasionally they are mustered and domesticated for use as working stock horses on farms or stations, but also as trail horses, show horses, Pony Club mounts and pleasure horses. These horses are the subject of some controversy, sometimes regarded as a pest and threat to native ecosystems, but valued by others as part of Australia's heritage, with supporters who work to prevent inhumane treatment or extermination. Several voluntary organisations also work to rehome captured Brumbies.

AUSTRALIAN PONY

The Australian Pony is a breed of pony that developed in as its name suggests, in Australia. Since the continent had no native horses or ponies prior to the arrival of European explorers and settlers, all equidae that now live there are from imported stock. Horses first arrived in Australia in 1788 on the ship First Fleet from South Africa. In 1803, the first Timor Ponies arrived from Indonesia, and provided the foundation stock for the breed. The Australian Pony also had later influence from the Welsh Mountain Pony, Hackney pony, Arabian, Shetland Pony, Highland Pony, Connemara Pony, Exmoor Pony, and from small Thoroughbreds. By 1920, a distinct type of pony had emerged in Australia, and in 1931, the Australian Pony Stud Book Society was formed. Today, the pony is mainly used as a children's mount and for smaller adult novice riders. They compete in dressage, eventing, show jumping, combined driving, gymkhana, mounted games, and horse shows.

The head of the breed, should show quality, with alert well proportioned ears, flat forehead, large dark well-filled eyes, with open nostrils. The head should be set on a well defined gullet. The neck should be slightly crested with good length with open nostrils. The head should be set on a well defined gullet. Shoulders should slope back to well defined withers. The shoulders should show no trace of heaviness or coarseness and the chest should be neither too narrow nor too wide.

BARB

Developed on the Barbary Coast of North Africa, the Barb is a desert horse, with great hardiness and stamina. Due to the amount of cross-breeding, it is difficult to find a pure-bred Barb today. The horses generally possess a fiery temperament and an atypical sport-horse conformation, but nevertheless has had an incredible impact on today's modern breeds. It is not exactly known where the Barb developed, but the breed originated in Northern Africa during the 8th century, about the time that Islamic invaders reached the region. There is considerable controversy over whether the Barb and Arabian horses share a common ancestor or if the Arabian was a predecessor of the Barb. It is possible that a native horse of the region was influenced by the crossing of multiple "oriental" breeds, including the Arabian horse, Turkmenian or Akhal-Teke, Caspian horse, with Iberian horses brought back from Europe by the Moorish invaders after they conquered southern Spain. Today there are several varieties of Barb, including the Algerina, Moroccan, and Tunisian. When imported to Europe, they were sometimes mistaken for Arabians, even though they have distinctly different characteristics, in part because their handlers were northern African Muslims who spoke Arabic. The Godolphin Arabian, which was one of the foundation sires for the thoroughbred breed, may have been a Barb stallion, and is sometimes called the Godolphin Barb. It is now bred primarily in Morocco, Algeria, Spain, and southern France, although, due to difficult economic times in its homeland, the number of pure-bred Barbs is decreasing. The World Organization of the Barb Horse, founded in Algeria in 1987, was formed to promote and preserve the breed. However, due to political situations, it is difficult to say how much of an increase in numbers or purity the breed will have.

BELGIAN HEAVY HORSE

The Belgian horse, Belgian Heavy Horse, or Brabant is a horse breed comes from the West-Brabantian region of Belgium. They are one of the strongest of the heavy breeds. The world's largest Belgian Horse was named Brooklyn Supreme, who weighed 3,200 pounds (a little over 1,450kg) and stood at 19.2 hands. On average the Belgian will grow to be slightly over 1 ton or 2,000 pounds. Colors normally are a type of light chestnut sometimes called a "sorrel," with a flaxen mane. They are considered a draft horse. Historically, though it is possible they may have had ancestors who were destriers in the Middle Ages, their main use was as a farm horse. They are still used as working animals, but have also become popular as show horses, gaming horses, and even as trail riding horses. Although the overall percentage of draft breeds among American horses has declined, the number of Belgians has increased.

The world's tallest living horse is a Belgian Draft named Radar. Radar is a gelding, born in 1998 in Iowa. He stands at 19.35 hands, which means he is approximately 6 foot 7 inches (2 metres) tall at the withers. He weighs over 2,400 lbs (1,088kg). He is currently used by Priefert Ranch Equipment for promotions. Importation of Belgians ended in bulk after the beginning of the Second World War with Erwin F. Dygert transporting the last Belgians out of Europe as the war was beginning. They are able to pull tremendous amounts of weight. At the National Western Stock Show in Denver, Colorado, a team of two horses in the Heavyweight class pulled 17,000 pounds 7'2". The team of Belgians weighed 4,800 pounds. At the Iowa State fair, the heavyweight champions in the pulling contest pulled 14,600 pounds the complete distance of 15'.

BUDYONNY

Budyonnys are very elegant warmblood horses with high withers, long legs and muscled neck and back. The head is noble, though often rather heavy and expressionate. In Russia, they are famous as showjumping horses. They also show excellent performance in long-distance races and have won steeplechase races as well. There are lines in the breed selected for shows and are tested in showjumping and dressage, whereas other lines do have more racehorse characteristics and are tested on the racetrack. Budyonny horses also have a lot of qualities that make them an excellent breed for hacking and leisure. In the big Russian studs such as the stud Budyonny and the stud of The First Cavalry Army (Pervaya Konnaya Armija), the horses are kept in large herds (called Tabun in Russian - not breed specific) who run free in the steppe. This guarantees healthy horses with good social behaviour and good movements.

Budyonnys have a lot of temperament. Kept in boxes, they often develop character problems. But when given enough space to run free, the horses show the calm, sensible side of their character. Budyonnys are "one-man horses" that need to have time to trust their owner. Due to their intelligence and surefootedness, they will have no problems with difficult grounds. The modern Budyonny is a horse of good height with a clean, solid build and heavily muscled body. The Budyonny is a good-tempered and energetic, an animal easily broken. The breed is well suited as a riding horse or for light carriage and is a good jumper. The Budyonny has free and easy movement at all gaits making it very well suited as a sporting horse for modern equestrian events.

CARMARGUE

The Camargue is an ancient breed of horses found in the Camargue area in Southern France. For centuries, possibly thousands of years, these small horses have lived wild in the harsh environment of the wetlands of the Rhone delta, the Camargue marshes, developing the stamina, hardiness and agility for which they are known today. Camargue horses are born black or dark brown in colour, but as they grow to adulthood, their coat lightens until it is pale grey or white. They are small horses, generally 13 to 14 hands high. Despite their small size, they have the strength to carry grown men. Rugged and intelligent, they have a short neck, deep chest, compact body, well-jointed, strong limbs, and a full mane and tail. Their calm temperament, agility, intelligence and stamina has resulted in these horses being used for equestrian games, dressage, and long distance riding, which is growing in popularity in France.

The Camargue breed was well appreciated by the Celtic and Roman invaders that entered the Iberian Peninsula, and as a result this genealogy is closely tied with Spanish breeds especially those in the northern part of the peninsula. The original Spanish "jaca" was probably a cross between the Celtic Pony and the Camargue and it was later improved further by crosses with northern European horse types and ultimately with the southern peninsular horse as the Moors spread their influence towards the Pyrenees. As a result, the Camargue genes very probably penetrated America through the influence of the "jaca" warhorses that were taken to these inhospitable lands where hardiness was a requirement. Breeds such as the Chilean Horse and Criollo show signs of some characteristics that are common in the Camargue breed.

CLEVELAND BAY

Believed to be the oldest breed in Britain (besides the native ponies), the Cleveland Bay was bred in the Cleveland area of north-eastern England. The foundation stock is said to have dated back to the times of the Romans, and there are record suggesting that the breed was in existence in medieval times. They were originally known as Chapman Horses, since they were used as pack horses for travelling salesmen known locally as 'chapmen'. As its name suggests, the Cleveland Bay is always a bay horse. No other color is allowed except a small white star and some white in the mane and tail. They are generally 16-16.2hh (63-65"), and have a good temperament. They have a long, sloping shoulder, strong limbs with plenty of bone, a strong back and hindquarter, and a large head with a fairly straight face. The Pure-Bred Cleveland Bay is a very intelligent horse with a sensible temperament. They possess a strong character which, if mishandled can be spoiled.

They have plenty of bone and substance, are hardy, long lived and have tremendous stamina. Characteristically the breed is very bold and honest. They are an established breed and so breed true to type. Their characteristics and traits are passed on to their progeny. This makes them an ideal out-cross. America, Japan, India, Australia and New Zealand and many other countries have imported Cleveland Bays to improve their native stock. Many European Warmbloods, particularly the Gelderlander, Oldenburg, Holstein, and Hanoverian owe much to the Cleveland Bay influence.

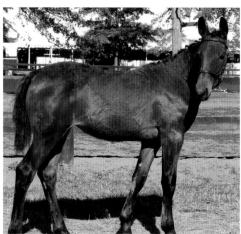

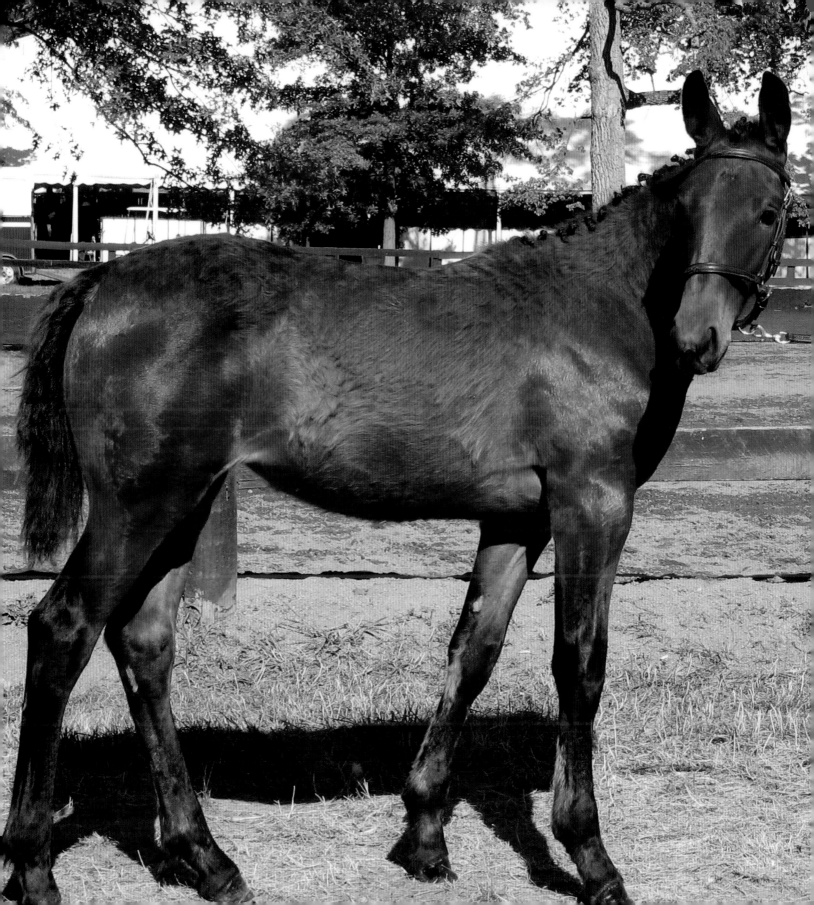

CLYDESDALE

The Clydesdale is a breed of draft horse derived from the very hard-working farm horses of Clydesdale, Scotland, and named for that region. Thought to be over 300 years old, the breed was extensively used for pulling heavy loads in rural, industrial and urban settings, their common use extending into the 1960s when they were still a familiar sight pulling the carts of milk and vegetable vendors. Clydesdales are noted for their rugged grace and versatility; they are strong yet amiable animals exceeding 18 hands (1.8 meters or 6 feet) in height and over one ton (1 Ton) in weight. A Clydesdale has a large head with somewhat arched profile, or Roman-nose, small ears, intelligent eyes and profuse forelock. The neck is generally straight, the chest deep, the shoulders with a lot of heavy bone. The back is rather short and a little curved, the withers high and the rump presenting a distinctively rounded silhouette. The legs should be long and strong with characteristically large hoof size, being about twice the width of a Thoroughbred race horse. The characteristic action of a Clydesdale is demonstrated at a trot. Clydesdales may be of several possible colors, including various shades of bay (sometimes called brown), roan, chestnut (sometimes called sorrel), and black.

Clydesdales have a range of characteristic white markings which are generally present regardless of body colour. The most distinctive are four white feet and a blaze, most often a full blaze or large, white "bald face" marking which extends to the lips and chin and may also extend to the eye region. Horses with white muzzles often have distinctive black spots around the lips and chin.

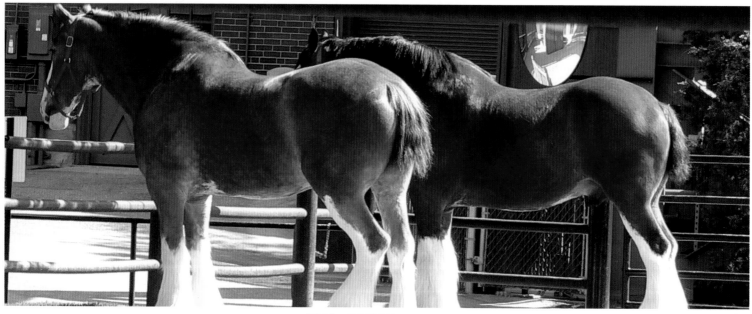

CRIOULO

The crioulo (in Portuguese) or "criollo" (in Spanish) is the native horse of Argentina, Uruguay, Brazil and Paraguay. It may have the best endurance of any horse breed in the world next to the Arabian. In fact, due to the crioulo's low basal metabolism it may be a better long distance horse than the Arabian in prolonged races over a week in duration with no supplemental feed. The breed is most popularly known for its hardiness and stamina.

The crioulo is a hardy horse with a brawny and strong body. They have short, strong legs with good bone, resistant joints, low set hocks, and sound, hard feet. The long muzzled head is medium to large sized and has a straight or slightly convex profile with wide-set eyes. The croup is sloping and the haunches well-muscled, the back short with a strong loin. They have sloping, strong shoulders with muscular necks. The body is deep with a broad chest and well-sprung ribs. The crioulo horses average 1.45 m (14.1 hh). The maximum height for stallions and geldings is 1.50 m (14.3 hh) high and the minimum height is 1.38 m (13.2 hh). The maximum and minimum heights for mares are 2 cm less (approximately one inch). The line backed dun is the most popular color, but the breed may also come in bay, brown, black, chestnut, grulla, buckskin, palomino, blue or strawberry roan, gray and overo colors. The breed dates back to a 1535 shipment of 100 Spanish stallions and mares to Rio de la Plata imported by Buenos Aires founder, Pedro de Mendoza. Although it has always been claimed the crioulo has a lot of Barb influence they may also have Southern Peninsular horse, Sorraia, Garrano and Castilian genes.

FREIBERGER

The Freiberger is a draft horse from Switzerland. It is the last representative of the light cold blood horse in Europe. Each year at the Marché Concours in Saignelégier, on the second weekend in August, Freiberger demonstrate how versatile they are in a variety of shows and competitions. Due to its character, willingness, and versatility, suitable for both driving and riding, it is a popular mount. They are also known as the Franches-Montagnes. The breed developed by crossing the native Bernese Jura horse with the English Thoroughbred type and Anglo-Norman, and also with the Ardennais and the Arab. There are two distinct types within the Freiberger breed: a broader, heavier stamp of horse with more muscle development and a lighter, finer type. Nowadays, there is a trend towards breeding the lighter type, as interest in competitive riding and leisure riding increases.

These days found in Italy as well as all over Europe, the Freiberger is a highly versatile horse, used for light draft, farm work, riding, and competitive riding. They are a mountain horse and do very well in hilly and mountainous areas, being naturally sure-footed and tough and, in many cases, far better equipped for working this type of land than a tractor. Typically, they have a heavy, although small, head with a pronounced jaw line and a broad forehead. The neck should be arched and muscular, with a good sloping shoulder, broad and pronounced withers, and a straight and powerful back. They invariably have good clean legs, strong joints, and hard feet. Traditionally, they had a very small amount of feathering at the fetlock, although modern breeding has largely bred this out, and they also have a somewhat finer head now, which sometimes shows Arabian character in the facial expressions.

FRIESIAN

The Friesian (also Frisian) horse is a breed of horse from Friesland, a province of the Netherlands. Although the breed's conformation resembles that of a light draft horse, Friesians are graceful and nimble for their size. During the Middle Ages, the ancestors of Friesian horses were in great demand as war horses throughout continental Europe. Though the breed nearly became extinct on more than one occasion, the modern day Friesian horse is growing in numbers and popularity, used both in harness and under saddle.

The Friesian is most often recognized by its black coat color, though color alone is not their only distinguishing characteristic. Friesians also have a long, thick mane and tail, and "feather"-long, silky hair on the lower legs, deliberately left untrimmed. The official breed rarely has white markings of any kind; most registries allow only a small star on the forehead for purebred registration. The Friesian's average height is about 15.3 hands (1.60 m), although it may vary from 14.2 to 17 hands (between 1.5 m and 1.7 m) tall at the withers, and mares must be at least 15.2 hands (1.57 m) tall to qualify for a special 'star-designation' pedigree. The breed is known for a fast, high-stepping trot. The Friesian is considered a willing, active, and energetic horse that is also gentle and docile. The breed has powerful overall conformation and good bone structure, with what is sometimes called a Baroque body type. Friesians have long, arched necks and well-chiselled, short-eared, "Spanish type" heads. Their sloping shoulders are quite powerful. They have compact, muscular bodies with strong sloping hindquarters and a low-set tail. Their limbs are comparatively short and strong.

HAFLINGER

Haflingers range in colour from a light gold to a rich golden chestnut or chocolate hue with a white or flaxen mane and tail. The desirable height for the breed is between 13.2 hands (138 cm) and 14.3 hands (150cm), although they can be up to 15 hands. The horse's appearance should be elegant and harmonious, with a refined and expressive head with large eyes, a well shaped mid-section, and a well-shaped croup which must not be too steep or too short. The horse should be well muscled and show correct, clean limbs with well formed clearly defined joints. Breeding stallions should have unmistakable masculine features and brood mares should exhibit undeniable feminine lines and features. The head should be noble and lean and should fit well with the rest of the horse. The eyes should be large and positioned forward. The neck is of medium length and should become narrower towards the head. There should be sufficient freedom through the jowls.

The legs should show clear, lean distinct joints, and equal stance on all four feet. Legs should be in a straight line when viewed front or back. From the side the front legs should be straight and hind legs should display an angle of 150 degrees through the hock and an angle of 45-50 degrees through the pastern and hoof to the ground. The knee should be broad and flat and the hocks wide and powerful. Pasterns should be long and well developed and the hooves should be round, distinct and hard. The Haflinger has diligent, rhythmic and ground covering gaits. The walk is relaxed, energetic, and proud and cadenced.

HANOVERIAN

A Hanoverian is a warmblooded horse originating in Germany, which is often seen in the Olympic Games and other difficult English style competitions, and have won gold medals in all three equestrian Olympic competitions. It is one of the oldest, most numerous, and most successful of the warmbloods. Originally a carriage horse, infusions of Thoroughbred blood lightened it to make it more agile and useful for competition. The Hanoverian is known for its wonderful temperament, athleticism, beauty, and grace.

The Hanoverian is said to have dated to the war-horse of the middle ages. In 1735, George II, the King of England and Elector of Hanover, founded the state stud at Celle. He began a breeding program for horses for use in agriculture and work in carriages. Selected stallions, many privately owned, were available to the local farmers for breeding. The bigger of the local mares were refined with Holsteins, Thoroughbreds and Cleveland Bays, and later some Neopolitan, Andalusian, Prussian, and Mecklenburg stock. By the end of the 18th century, the Hanoverian had become a high-class coach horse.

The horses are elegant, strong, and robust. They are bred to be willing and trainable, and have a strong back, powerful body, athletic movement, and strong limbs. Chestnut, bay, brown, black, and gray are found the most often. Regulations prohibit horses with too much white, and buckskin, palomino and cremello horses from being registered. The horses can be 15.3-17.2 hands high, but most are in the range of 16-16.2 hands.

HIGHLAND PONY

The Highland Pony is a native British pony, and is the largest of Britain's 9 native breeds. Its pedigree dates back to the 1880s. It was once a workhorse in the Scottish mainland and islands, but today is used for trekking and general riding. The height is 13hh to 14.2hh. Head should be well-carried and alert with a kindly eye, broad muzzle and deep jowl. Reasonable length of neck going from wither with a good sloping shoulder and well-placed forearm. Well-balanced and compact body with deep chest. Ribs well sprung. Powerful quarters with well-developed thigh, strong second thigh and clean flat hocks. Flat hard bone, broad knees, short cannon bones, oblique pasterns and well-shaped broad dark hoofs. Feather hair at back of legs soft and silky. Mane and tail should be natural, flowing and untrimmed. A range of duns - mouse, yellow, grey, cream. Also grey, brown, black and occasionally bay and liver chestnut with silver mane and tail. Many ponies have a dorsal stripe and some show zebra markings on legs. Shoulder stripe often present. A small star is acceptable but other white markings are discouraged. Foal coat often changes and many ponies change colour gradually as they grow older, especially those with grey hairs interspersed with the original colour. Others show a slight seasonal change in colour between winter and summer coats. Broken colours are not allowed. Stallions with white markings other than a small star are not eligible for licensing by the Highland Pony Society. No white markings (other than a small star) nor white legs or white hoofs are acceptable in the showring. The Highland Pony Society actively discourages white markings of any description other than a small white star.

HOLSTEIN

The Holstein is a breed of horse originating in the Schleswig-Holstein region of northern Germany. It is thought to be the oldest of warmblood breeds, tracing back to the 13th century. The Holsteiners usually are a bay, dark bay, or black (although other colors are found) and are 16-17 hands high. They have powerful hindquarters, making them great at show jumping, with strong bone, excellent movement (needed for dressage), and sloping shoulders, making them great gallopers. They generally have strong limbs, a long, crested neck, and strong feet. They have a broad back and a well set tail. The Schleswig-Holstein marshlands of Germany have been breeding horses since 1225. It was famous for its war horses in the middle ages, and then, in the 16th to 18th century bred popular coach horses after refining their horses with Spanish, Neapolitan, and Barbary blood. In the 19th century, the demand for a faster coach horse and for a lighter cavalry horse encouraged the breeders to lighten the breed with British Stallions. The most influential were three Yorkshire Coach Horses, all of which traced back to the Thoroughbred stallion Eclipse. They made the Holstein into a high-stepping carriage horse, as well as a horse strong enough for agricultural work.

In the 1960s, the Holstein was refined yet again, using Thoroughbreds. Most were imported from Britain and Ireland, and they were used to make the breed more athletic. Holstein blood has been infused in many other sport horse breeds, including Dutch, Danish, and British Warmbloods. Today, the Holstein is high in demand, especially in dressage and showjumping.

ICELANDIC

The Icelandic Horse is a man-made breed as it is a mixture of breeds and cross-breeds which were taken from Scandinavian and European countries to Iceland during the original and subsequent settlements. Because they are by-and-large pony-sized, they are commonly called "Icelandic ponies" in some countries. There are roughly 80,000 Icelandic horses in Iceland, and relatively few abroad, owing in large part to centuries-old Icelandic legislation that prevents any Icelandic horse from returning to the island once it has been taken to another land. They are considered small (average 13 horse hands high, or 4'4", or about 1.20 to 1.45m, roughly 800 pounds) but very strong for their size. They can carry roughly one-third of their weight, but have to be about four-years-old before they can carry a full-sized adult male human. The only work they are used for is rounding up sheep from the highlands and herding livestock (sheep, cattle and horses) on farms. Most horses are mainly used for leisure riding, gaited competition, and for an Icelandic brand of horse-racing. Icelandic horses are known for their special gaits. Apart from walk, trot and canter, Icelandic horses are able to tölt and some can go in skei (pace). Skei is a gait where the horse moves both legs of one side at the same time; it is considered a gait for racing, and ridden at the proper speed is called flugskei, loosely translated as "flying pace". A slow pace, like that used in riding certain Peruvian horse breeds, is considered undesirable in Icelandic horses, and is called lull (piggy pace). It is thought that Icelandic horses have become about 10 cm higher during the second half of the 20th century, but that probably has less to do with selective breeding and more to do with increased quality of fodder. However, one of the breeding goals is to have a taller, more refined horse.

LIPIZZANER

The Lipizzan, or Lipizzaner (Slovene Lipicanec), is a breed of horse closely associated with the Spanish Riding School of Vienna, Austria where the finest representatives demonstrate the "high school" movements of classical dressage, including the highly advanced "airs above the ground." The Lipizzan breed dates back to the 16th century, when it was developed with the support of the Habsburg nobility. The breed takes its name from one of the earliest stud farms established, located near the Kras village of Lipica (spelled "Lipizza" in Italian), in modern-day Slovenia. Most Lipizzans measure between 15 and sixteen hands. They are compact and muscular, with very powerful hindquarters, allowing them to do the difficult "High School" (Dressage) movements, including the "airs above the ground." They generally have a strong-featured head with a convex profile, set high on a well-muscled, arched neck. They have short cannons, their legs have good bone, and well-sloped shoulders. Their gaits are powerful and elastic, although different in style from the Warmblood breeds seen in many Dressage competitions. Lipizzans are naturally balanced, well-known for excellent trainability and intelligence. Lipizzan stallions are still the "Dancing White Horses," the only horses used by the Spanish Riding School in Vienna. Both purebred and crossbred Lipizzans make excellent riding and harness horses. While popular for dressage exhibitions and recreational riding in Europe and North America, in some countries (such as Slovenia) stallions are crossed with local mares to make good farm horses in addition to being used for dressage.

LUSITANO

The Lusitano is an ancient Portuguese breed of horse that until the 1960s shared its registration with the Spanish horse, the Andalusian. Both are sometimes called Iberian horses, as their land of origin is the Iberian peninsula. These Iberian horses were developed for use in war, dressage and bull fighting.Lusitanos make excellent riding horses due to their levelheaded temperament and tendency to bond strongly with humans. They are intelligent, sensible, and have great balance.Lusitano are extremely proficient at the high levels of dressage; including the high-school movements of piaffe, passage, pirouettes, flying lead changes and half pass. The Lusitano is also noted to have very comfortable gaits. Not unlike the famous Lipizzans, many Lusitanos turn white with age. They come in a striking variety of solid colors and usually stand 15 to 16 hands. The Palomino and Cremello Lusitano are the most rare and most sought after. They are compact, with powerful hindquarters, some with high-stepping action, and a thick mane and tail. They have a Roman nose with a wide forehead. They also have a sloping croup and low-set tail, as well as short backs. They have a low set cresty neck, a broad chest, well-sprung ribs. They are extremely powerful and strong, due to their muscular hindquarters and strong, long legs.In America Lusitanos and Andalusians are registered together under the International Andalusian and Lusitano Horse Association (IALHA.)

MANGALARGA MARCHADOR

The Mangalarga Marchador is a breed of horse. Highly regarded as the National Horse, there are over 350,000 registered Mangalarga Marchador horses in Brazil and a number found in several countries outside its Brazilian homeland. As an Iberian breed, descending from the Andalusian horse stallions of Portugal and barb mares, they have carriage, beauty and intelligence, a warm personality and are easily trained for almost any discipline. The Marchador horses are known for having a smooth stable walk, canter and gallop as well as a natural diagonal (batida) or lateral (picada) four beat gait with a brief moment of triple hoof support. Their endurance, versatility out on the range, trail and pleasure riding as well as the ability to be trained in dressage or jump, makes the batida Mangalarga Marchador a wonderful sport horse that can be inspected and registered as a warmblood.

While there are less than two hundred foundation Mangalarga Marchador horses in the United States, they are catching the attention of the horse world. The breed is of middle size, agile, strong structures and well proportionate, vigorous and healthy, visually light expression in the appearance, fine and smooth skin, fine, smooth and silky furry, active and docile temperament.

The ideal height for males is of 1,52m, when there are admitted for the definite register at least 1,47m and maxim of 1,57m. For females ideal is of 1,46m, when there are admitted for the definite register at least 1,40m and maxim of 1,54m.

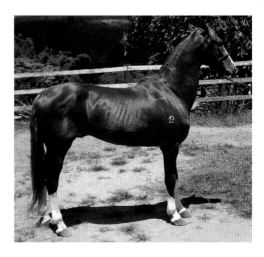

MAREMMANO

The Maremmano horse breed is bred in Tuscany, Italy and gets its name from Maremma a coastal tract on the Tyrrhenian Sea. This horse breed whose origins are not completely known was the mount of the Italian Army and has always been a favorite with local farmers and cowboys. Arab, Barb, Norfolk Roadster and more recently the Thoroughbred horse breeds are likely to have influenced the Maremmano horse. The Maremmano is believed to be descended from the Neopolitan horses which were made famous in the sixteenth century by Federico Grisone, the founder of the Neopolitan Riding Academy. Grisone was considered to be the first of the great clasical ridng masters after the Greek, Xenophon. These horses are good honest workers, which are calm and tough. They make good army, police and cattle horses. The Maremmano horse breed stands 15.3hh and can be any solid color. They are somewhat coarse in appearance with upright shoulders and flat withers. They are usually around 15.3 hh. In other words, 61.2 in. They can be of any solid color. The have flat withers and a quite low-set tail. There is an annual show in Canino, Italy which represents, among other things, an homage made by institutions to breeders of maremmano horses who have, with great sacrifices, preserved and improved a breed of great prestige and very ancient traditions (it was employed by the Etruscans). It also means to pay homage to a mythical figure in the Maremma of Tuscany and Lazio: the butteri, local cowboys who are still fundamental in cattle and horse farming. The schedule of the show will be full of events: horse shows, performance tests and a regional show on maremmano horses.

MUSTANG

A Mustang is a hardy, free-roaming horse of the North American west, descended primarily from horses brought to the Americas by the Spanish conquistadores. In 1971, the United States Congress recognized Mustangs as "living symbols of the historic and pioneer spirit of the West," which continue to "contribute to the diversity of life forms within the Nation and enrich the lives of the American people." The first Mustangs descended from Iberian horses brought to Mexico in the 1500s by the Conquistadores. Most of these horses were of Andalusian, Arabian and Barb ancestry. Some of these horses escaped or were stolen by Native Americans, and rapidly spread throughout western North America. Native Americans quickly adopted the horse as a primary means of transportation. Many tribes bred their horses carefully to improve them for their purposes. Among the most capable horse-breeding people of North America were the Comanche, the Shoshoni, and the Nez Perce. The latter in particular became master horse breeders, and developed one of the first truly American breeds: the Appaloosa. The Bureau of Land Management is tasked with protecting, managing, and controlling wild horses and burros under the authority of the 1971 Wild Free-Roaming Horses and Burros Act to ensure that healthy herds thrive on healthy rangelands and as multiple-use mission under the 1976 Federal Land Policy and Management Act. Today, free-roaming horses have disappeared from 6 states and, according to the Bureau of Land Management (BLM), their remaining population is fewer than 25,000, with more than half of them in Nevada, with other significant populations in Montana, and Oregon. A few hundred free-roaming horses survive in Alberta and British Columbia.

NEW FOREST PONY

The New Forest Pony is one of the recognised nine Mountain and Moorland or Native pony breeds of the British Isles, valued for its hardiness, strength and sureness of foot. Many of them can be seen running loose on the New Forest in southern England; although the ponies may appear wild (which they are to some extent), they are privately owned by Commoners of the New Forest. The ponies are looked after by their owners and the Agisters (employees of the Verderers of the New Forest). The Verderers are a modern statutory body with ancient roots, that shares the management of the forest with the Forestry Commission. There have been references to the New Forest pony as far back as 1016. Stud books have been in existence since 1906. Thoroughbred and Arab blood has been introduced into the breed from time to time to improve looks and increase height. The areas of the forest occupied by discrete groups of ponies are commonly called "haunts". The upper height limit is 148 cm. There is no lower limit but New Forest ponies are seldom under 12 hands (120 cm). They are normally shown in two height sections 138 cm and under (competition type A) and over 138 cm (competition height B). The New Forest pony may be any colour except piebald, skewbald or blue-eyed cream. Palomino or very light chestnut and cream ponies with dark eyes are only acceptable as geldings and mares. Blue eyes are not permitted. New Forest ponies should be of riding type with substance. They should have sloping shoulders, strong quarters, plenty of bone, good depth of body, straight limbs and good hard round feet. The larger ponies, while narrow enough for small children are quite capable of carrying adults. The smaller ponies, though not up to so much weight, often show more show quality.

NORWEGIAN FJORD

The Fjord horse (known in Norway as a fjording) is a rather short but very strong breed of horse from the mountainous regions of western Norway. It ranges from 137 to 147 centimetres (approximately 13.2 to 14.2 hands) in height and weighs from 400 to 550 kilograms (about 882 to 1210 lb), which classifies it as a pony according to international rules (though it is always called a horse in Norway). It has a strong neck, good feet, and a compact, muscular body. It is always dun in color, brown dun being the most common. The Fjord also comes in three other varieties of Dun (color); grey, red, white and the extremely rare yellow. It has small brown marks over the eyes and on the checks and thighs. The ears bear dark outlines and tips. There is some "feathering" on the legs, and occasionally zebra-like dark horizontal stripes. The coat is thin and shiny in summer, but longer and furry in winter. The mane is long, thick, and heavy, but is usually clipped to between five to ten centimeters (two to four inches) so that it stands up, making grooming easier and accentuating the horse's strong neck and full-length dorsal stripe. In few other breeds does the dorsal stripe extend all the way from poll to tail. The fjord horse is a favourite at Norwegian riding and therapeutic schools, as its generally mild temperament and small size make it suitable for children and disabled individuals. It has also been used as a sport horse. Its ability to handle difficult terrain has led to achievement in show jumping and dressage where they have reached the highest levels. They are considered very good driving horses, and are commonly used in everything from competitions to tourist transport in Norway. Fjord horses were used in mountainous terrain during WWII, and also served as food during the food shortages in the Netherlands in 1944-1945.

OLDENBURG

The Oldenburg was first bred in Lower Saxony, Germany. The foundations were first laid by Count Johan von Oldenburg in the late 16th century. He bred Friesian mares with Danish, Turkish, Neopolitan, and Andalusian stallions to produce large war horses. His son, Count Anton, travelled Europe and brought home the finest Spanish and Italian stallions, to add speed and strength. His tenant farmers were also allowed to breed from his stallions, establishing the tradition of small, private studs that is still common with the breeders in that region today.

In the 17th century, the Oldenburg became a well-known coach horse, admired for its height, power, and elegance. To be approved for breeding, a stallion must be certified by a licensing commission from the Oldenburg breed society. Several hundred horses are inspected at the age of 2.5, and the best 75-85 horses are then placed through a 3-day test, judged on their conformation and type. On the final day, the best of this smaller group are then chosen to be graded, with the most excellent earning the title of "Premium Stallion." The graded horses are then taken to a 100-day testing, which judges the stallions on performance. This includes temperament, rideability, jumping ability, endurance, speed, and movement. Poor performance will prevent the horse from being approved for the final breeding stock status. Overall scores plus pedigree requirements dictate which book the mares will enter into. Foals are inspected as sucklings or weanlings for foal papers, their original pink papers which verify parentage and breeding.

The Oldenburg Verband (Oldenburg Horse Breeders Society) is the original registry for Oldenburger horses world wide.

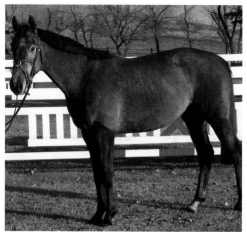
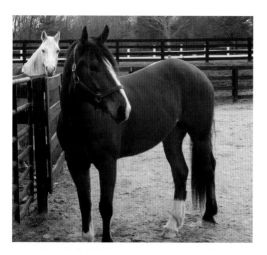

PAINT HORSE

The American Paint Horse is a breed of horse that combines both the conformational characteristics of a western stock horse with a pinto spotting pattern of white and dark coat colors. Developed from a base of spotted horses with Quarter Horse and Thoroughbred bloodlines, the American Paint Horse is now one of the fastest-growing breeds in the United States. American Paint Horses have strict bloodline requirements and a distinctive stock-horse body type. To be eligible for registry, a Paint's sire and dam must be registered with the American Paint Horse Association, the American Quarter Horse Association, or the Jockey Club (Thoroughbreds). At least one of the parents must be a registered American Paint Horse. In addition to bloodlines, to be eligible for the Regular Registry of the American Paint Horse Association (APHA), the horse must also exhibit a "natural Paint marking," meaning either a predominant hair coat color with at least one contrasting area of solid white hair of the required size with some underlying unpigmented skin present on the horse at the time of its birth. Or, in the case of a predominantly white hair coat, at least one contrasting area of the required size of colored hair with some underlying pigmented skin present on the horse. Natural Paint markings usually must cover more than two inches and be located in certain designated areas of the body.

Solid colored offspring of two registered Paint parents, called "Solid Paint-Breds" or "Breeding Stock Paints," are also eligible for registration, with certain restrictions. They are not able to participate in some recognized Paint breed shows, but there are alternative programs offered, and many incentive programs within the registry are available to Solid Paint-bred horses.

PALOMINO

Palomino is a coat color in horses, consisting of a gold coat and white or flaxen mane and tail. Genetically, the palomino color is created by a dilution gene working on a red (chestnut) base coat. However, most color breed registries that record Palomino horses were founded before equine coat color genetics were understood as well as they are today, and hence the standard definition of a Palomino is based on the coat color visible to the eye, not the underlying presence of the dilution gene. While the breed standard states the ideal color is that of a "newly minted gold coin" (sometimes mistakenly claimed to be a penny), some Palomino registries allow a coat color that may range from cremello, an almost-white color, to a deep, dark, chocolate color ("chocolate palomino"). Skin and eyes are usually dark. White markings are permitted on the legs, but must not extend beyond the knees or hocks. White markings are also permitted on the face, but must not extend past the eyes. Those with a chocolate colored coat may be confused with horses expressing the silver dapple gene. The Palomino is considered a color breed. Unlike the Appaloosa, which is a distinct breed that also happens to have a unique color, any breed or type of horse usually may be registered as palomino if they are properly golden-colored (though, for some registries, horses may also meet a conformation or type standard). The palomino is not a true breed, however, because palomino color does not breed "true;" A palomino crossed with a palomino may result in a palomino (about 50% of the time), but could also produce a chestnut (25%) or a cremello (25%). Thus, palomino is simply a color and not a set of characteristics that make up a "breed."

PERCHERON

Percherons serve as logging horses but also are valued as pleasure driving horses, riding horses, and as competitors in both regular horse shows and in draft horse showing.

Percherons are noted for heavy muscling and for an aspect of ruggedness and power. Also characteristic of the Percheron is clean action and quality conformation of the feet and legs. The mane is thick, though the tail is usually cut short. The breed is close coupled, wide and deep through the chest, with plenty of back rib. The muscles of the forearms, croup and gaskins are especially emphasized in a good drafter, and ease and balance of gait is essential. The Percheron head and neck is typical of the correct draft horse. Good Percherons have a large and full prominent eye, a broad and full forehead, and straight face. A wide jaw and refined ears attractively set and carried with animation are visible evidence of the Percheron's Arabian ancestry. Stallions should have a ruggedness about the head and mares should have a feminine look. The neck is well-shaped and powerful Percherons have withers well defined, a short back, a deep girth, long, somewhat level croup, big, well-rounded hip, and powerful mucsling in the lower thigh.In recent years, modern show Percherons have been bred for a longer, thinner neck, a longer back, and longer, smoother-looking muscles. These types of modern percherons are used mainly as show horses for competition.They are generally very gentle horses, well-suited for driving, and are strong and willing workers. The Percheron is readily adapted to varying climates and conditions. They have the strength to pull heavy loads and the graceful style to pull a fine carriage.

ROCKY MOUNTAIN

Around the turn of the century, a young horse soon to be called the Rocky Mountain Horse appeared in eastern Kentucky that gave rise to a line of horses prized by North American and European owners. On the farm of Sam Tuttle in Spout Springs Kentucky, there stood a stallion "Old Tobe". This sure footed, gentle horse carried young, old, and inexperienced riders over the rugged mountain trails of Natural Bridge State Park where Sam held the concession for horse-back riding. Even though Old Tobe was a breeding stallion, he carried riders without faltering. He fathered many fine horses up until the age of 37, and many of the present Rocky Mountain Horses carry his bloodline.

The basic characteristics of the breed are a medium sized horse of gentle temperament with an easy-ambling four-beat gait. This gait made it the horse of choice on the farms and rugged foothills of the Appalachian Mountains. It was a horse for all seasons. It could pull the plows in the small fields, work cattle, be ridden bareback, or be hitched up to a buggy. Because of its rugged upbringing it tolerated the winters in Kentucky with a minimum of shelter. Naturally, outcrossing with local horses did occur, but the basic characteristics of a strong genetic line have continued.

In the summer of 1986, as a way of preserving the breed, a number of people got together to form the Rocky Mountain Horse Association (RMHA) as a non-profit corporation in the state of Kentucky. The association established a breed registry and formed a panel of examiners to provide vigorous supervision to the growth and development of the breed.

SHIRE

The Shire horse is a breed of draught horse (UK) or draft horse (US). It is the tallest of the modern draught breeds, and a stallion may stand 18 or more hands (about 180 cm) high and weigh a short ton. The Shire horse has a dense rounded body, a broad back, strong loins, powerful hind-quarters, and long legs with dense bones. It can be black, brown, bay, or gray and has distinctive long silky hair (often white) on the lower parts of its legs. The hair down the back of the legs is called the "feather", while the hair over the foot is known as the "spats" The Shire horse descends from the medieval Great Horse brought to England in 1066 by William the Conqueror. From this medieval horse came a draught horse called the Black Horse in the seventeenth century, which was dull-colored and sluggish. The Black Horse was greatly improved by the followers of Robert Bakewell, resulting in a horse commonly known as the Bakewell Black. When the Pedigree Society was founded in 1878, the name was changed to English Cart Horse, since black was a misnomer. Six years later, the name was again changed to Shire. The breed was improved during the following years as ruthless veterinary examinations virtually eliminated the old unsoundness of wind and limb. With the increased use of mechanized farm and transport equipment, the numbers of Shire horses began to decline. By the middle of the twentieth century their numbers had dwindled to a small fraction of what they had been in their heyday. Numbers of Shires are on the rise again, however. They are now widely used in breeding heavier hunter types by crosses with thoroughbred mares, and are also seen in Draught or Draft horse competition worldwide.

STANDARDBRED

Standardbred harness racing horses are so called because in the early years of the Trotting Registry, the standardbred stud book established in the United States in 1879 by the National Association of Trotting Horse Breeders, only horses who could race a mile in a standard time or better, or whose get (offspring) could race a mile in standard time or better, were entered in the book. The first harness racehorses in North America were raced on the roads while going home to do the work on the farm or homestead. Contributing to the Standardbred breed were the Narragansett Pacer and the Canadian Pacer. Crosses between English Thoroughbreds and other breeds, including the Norfolk Trotter, the Hackney, the Morgan and the Canadian Pacer produced a horse that was the predecessor to the Standardbred. The stud book was formed in 1939, with the formation of the United States Trotting Horse Association. Standardbreds are known for their skill in harness racing, being the fastest trotting horse in the world. In continental Europe all harness races are conducted between trotters. A trotter's forelegs move in unison with the opposite hind legs — when the right foreleg moves forward so does the left hind leg, and vice versa. In Australia, Canada, New Zealand, the United Kingdom, and the United States, races are also held for pacers. Pacers' forelegs move in unison with the hind legs on the same side. Some of the major pacing races in North America include the Woodrow Wilson and Metro Stake for 2-year-olds, and the Little Brown Jug, Meadowlands Pace, North America Cup and the Adios for 3-year-olds. The Little Brown Jug, the Messenger Stake, and the Cane Pace comprise the Pacing Triple Crown.

  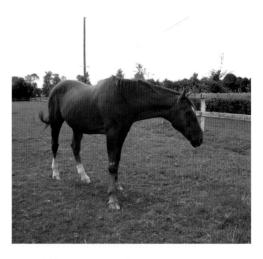

TRAKEHNER

Owing to its Thoroughbred ancestry, the Trakehner is of rectangular build, with a long sloping shoulder, good hindquarters, short cannons, and a medium-long, crested and well-set neck. The head is often finely chiseled, narrow at the muzzle, with a broad forehead. It is known for its "floating trot" - full of impulsion and suspension. The Trakehner possesses a strong, medium-length back and powerful hindquarters. Trakehners are athletic and trainable, with good endurance, while some are more spirited than horses of other warmblood breeds. Trakehners breed true to type, due to the purity of the bloodlines, making it valuable for upgrading other warmbloods. The breed's origins trace back to the native East Prussian Schwaike (now extinct), a small primitive horse first discovered by the Knights Templar in the 13th Century. Descendants of the Schwaike were used by East Prussian farmers for light utility work. In 1732 King Frederick William I of Prussia established the Main Stud Trakehnen at the East Prussian town Trakehnen (now Yasnaya Polyana, Russia). In the years between 1817 and 1837, the stud added Arabian, Thoroughbred, and Turkish blood to their horses. One especially influential Thoroughbred was Perfectionist, by Persimmon, who won the Epsom Derby and the St. Leger in 1896. He was to be the sire of the great Trakehner stallion Tempelhüter, and most modern Trakehners can be traced to these two stallions. The Arabian blood was added to offset possible flaws of the Thoroughbred. East Prussian farmers were encouraged to bring their mares, by then known for their hardness and quality, to Trakehnen's stallions, which allowed for the rapid transformation of the breed into much sought after army remounts; sure-footed, intelligent, and athletic.

WELSH PONY

The original Welsh Mountain Pony is thought to have evolved from the prehistoric Celtic pony. Welsh ponies were primarily developed in Wales and existed in the British Isles prior to the arrival of the Roman Empire. They were adapted to the difficult climate of severe winters and sparse vegetation. Shelter most often was an isolated valley or a clump of bare trees. Bands of ponies roamed in a semi-feral state climbing mountains, leaping ravines, running over rough terrain. Therefore the Welsh pony developed intelligence, speed and soundness, and is known for "heart" and endurance. They are tough and thrifty, with a steady, tractable, and calm nature. When the Romans occupied Ancient Britain, they brought horses of their own, which bred with the native ponies, producing hardy offspring with substance and attractive appearance. It is believed that Julius Caesar founded a stud for the ponies on the shores of Lake Bala. The characteristics of the breed as it is known today are thought to have been established by the late fifteenth century, after Crusaders returned to England with Arabian stallions obtained from the Middle East. In the 1500s, King Henry VIII, thinking to improve the breeds of horses, particularly war horses, ordered the destruction of all stallions under 15 hands and all mares under 13 hands. Fortunately the ponies in the wild, remote, and inaccessible mountains of Wales escaped this order. On the upland farms of Wales, Welsh ponies and cobs would often have to do everything from plowing a field to carrying a farmer to market or driving a family to church on Sunday. When coal mining became important to the economy of England, many Welsh ponies were used in mines, for pulling carts. In the eighteenth and nineteenth centuries, more Arabian blood was added by stallions who were turned out in the Welsh hills.

INDEX